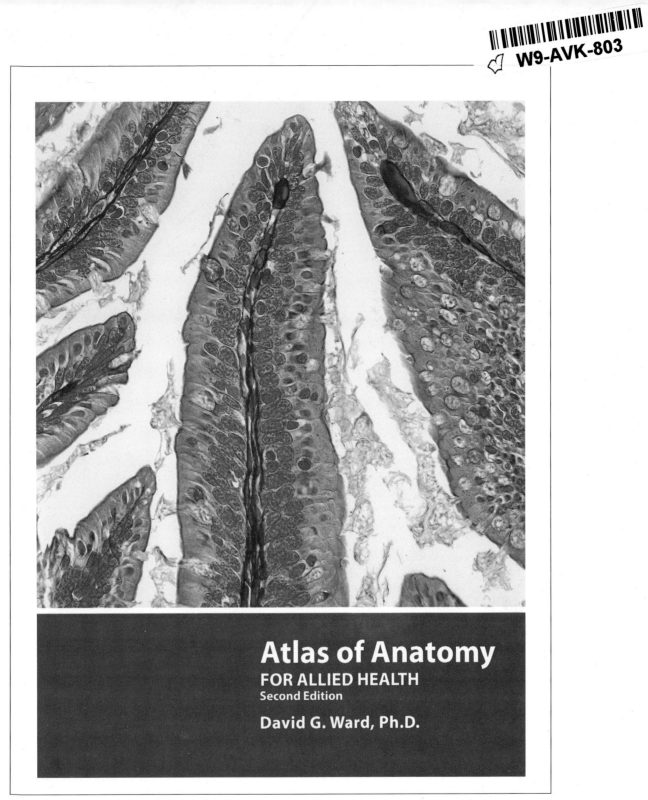

Atlas of Anatomy
FOR ALLIED HEALTH
Second Edition

David G. Ward, Ph.D.

small publishing done big™

ISBN-13: 978-1-59984-159-5
ISBN-10: 1-59984-159-2

© Cover images and illustration by the Author.
  Front cover: a photomicrograph of villi, goblet cells and mucus in the jejunum.
  Back cover upper right: a photomicrograph of lipids in adipocytes and collagen in the adipose tissue of the stomach.
  Back cover center: model of the exterior of the head.
  Back cover lower right: a photomicrograph of the lumen, transitional epithelium and smooth muscle in the ureter.

The models in this publication were photographed by the author and are manufactured by the following sources:
American 3B Scientific, Tucker, GA
Denoyer-Geppert International, Skokie, IL
SOMSO Modelle GMBH, Coburg, Germany

Published by bluedoor, LLC
        6595 Edenvale Boulevard, Suite 150
        Eden Prairie, MN 55346
        800-979-1624
        www.bluedoorpublishing.com

Printed in the United States of America.
10 9 8 7 6 5 4 3

Table of Contents

Section 7: Autonomic Nervous System, Endocrine Glands, and Reproductive Organs . . 7-1

Section 1

Cells, Epithelial and Connective Tissues and Skin

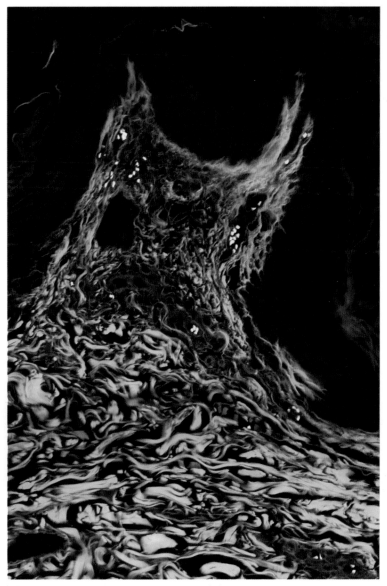

Fibrous connective tissue in dermis of skin (autofluorescence, x380)

Cells and Tissues

Mammalian Cell

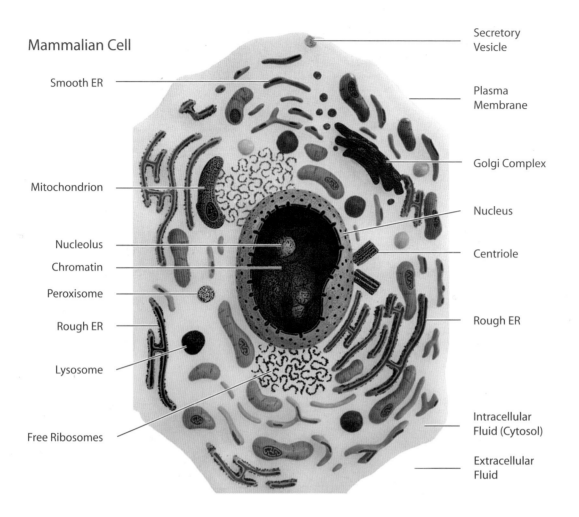

Secretory Vesicle

Smooth ER

Plasma Membrane

Golgi Complex

Mitochondrion

Nucleus

Nucleolus

Centriole

Chromatin

Peroxisome

Rough ER

Rough ER

Lysosome

Intracellular Fluid (Cytosol)

Free Ribosomes

Extracellular Fluid

Squamous epithelial cells

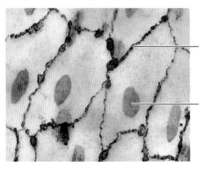

Plasma membrane

Nucleus

mesothelium (brightfield)

Glandular epithelial cell

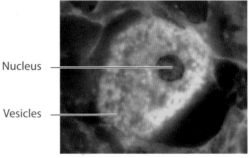

Nucleus

Vesicles

Parietal cell - stomach (fluorescence)

Mitosis

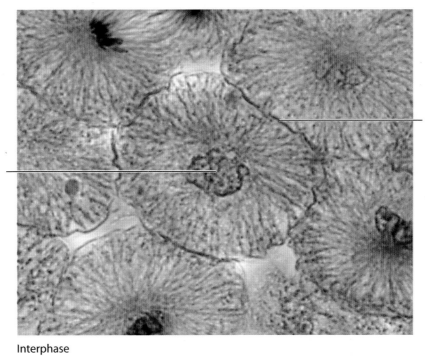

Nucleus

Plasma membrane

Interphase

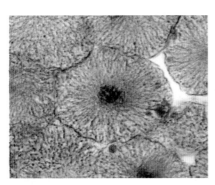

Prophase

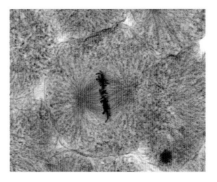

Metaphase

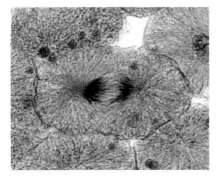

Anaphase

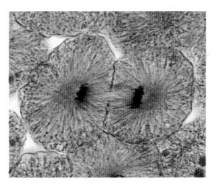

Telophase

Epithelial Tissues - Histology

Simple Squamous Epithelium

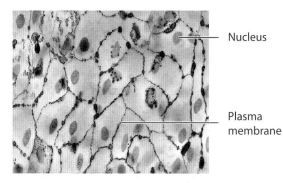

Nucleus

Plasma
membrane

Mesothelium of abdominal cavity-
surface view

Nuclei

Endocardium of heart - side view

Simple Cuboidal Epithelium

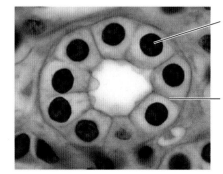

Nucleus

Plasma
membrane

Distal tubule of kidney

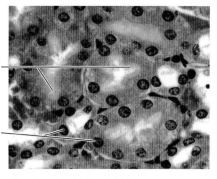

microvilli

Nuclei

Proximal tubule of kidney

Simple Columnar Epithelium

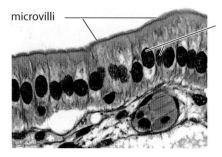

microvilli

Nuclei

Mucosa of small intestine

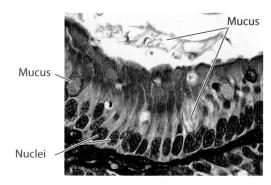

Mucus

Mucus

Nuclei

Mucosa of small intestine

Epithelial Tissues - Histology

Pseudostratified Ciliated Columnar Epithelium

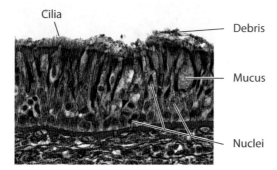

Cilia

Debris

Mucus

Nuclei

Mucosa of trachea

Transitional Epithelium

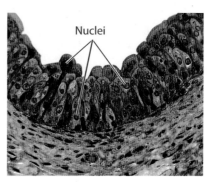

Nuclei

Mucosa of ureter

Stratified Squamous Epithelium - Keratinized

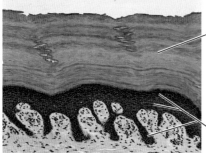

Dead cells

Nuclei

Epidermis of skin

Stratified Squamous Epithelium - Non-Keratinized

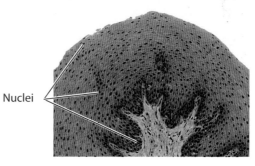

Nuclei

Mucosa of esophagus

Glandular Epithelium

Mucus in Goblet Cells

Nuclei

Goblet Cells of small intestine

Glandular Epithelium

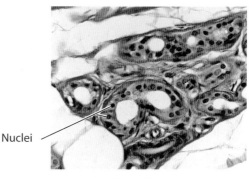

Nuclei

Sweat gland of skin

Connective Tissues - Histology

Areolar Fibrous

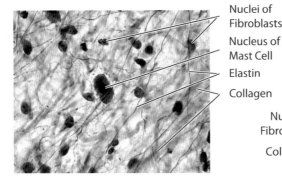

Nuclei of Fibroblasts
Nucleus of Mast Cell
Elastin
Collagen

Under epithelia

Dense Irregular Fibrous

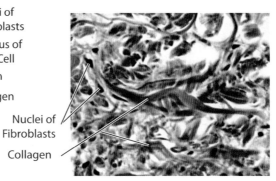

Nuclei of Fibroblasts
Collagen

Dermis of skin

Dense Regular Fibrous

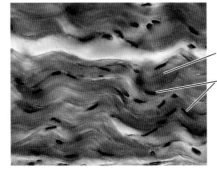

Collagen
Nuclei of Fibroblasts

Tendon

Elastic

Elastin

Nuclei of Fibroblasts

Internal elastic lamina of artery
(autofluorescence)

Hyaline Cartilage

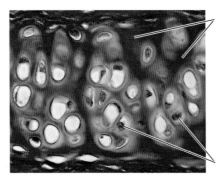

Chondroitin

Nuclei of Chondrocytes

Cartilage of trachea

Dense (Compact) Bone

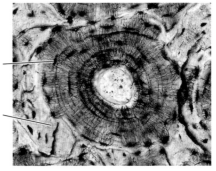

Nuclei of Osteocytes

Calcium Phosphate

Shaft of bone

Connective, Muscle, and Nervous Tissues -Histology

Adipose

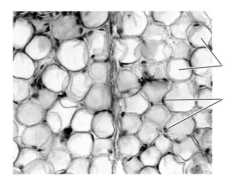

Lipids in
Adipocytes

Nuclei in
Adipocytes

Hypodermis of skin

Adipose

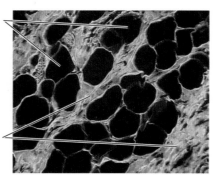

Lipids in
Adipocytes

Collagen

Around stomach (autofluorescence)

Adipose and Skeletal Muscle

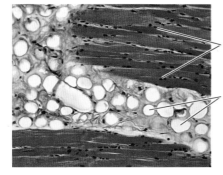

Nuclei in
skeletal
muscle cells

Lipids in
Adipocytes

Nuclei in
skeletal
muscle cells

Skeletal Muscle

Skeletal Muscle

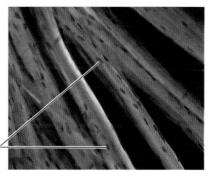

Nuclei in
skeletal
muscle cells

Skeletal muscle cells (polarized light)

Nervous

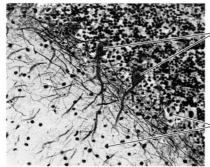

Nuclei of
Neurons

Nuclei of
Glial Cells

Purkinje cells in cerebellum

Nervous

Dendrite

Nuclei of
Neurons

Nucleus of
Multipolar
Neuron

Dendrite

Nuclei of
Glial Cells

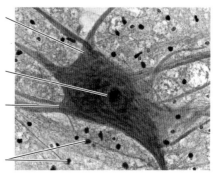

Motor neuron in spinal cord

Thick Skin and Scalp

Thick Skin

Sweat Duct
Stratum Corneum
Stratum Lucidum
Stratum Granulosum
Stratum Spinosum
Stratum Germinativum
Dermal Papilla
Tactile Corpuscle
Sweat Duct
Merocrine Sweat Gland
Lamellated Corpuscle

Epidermis
Dermis
Hypodermis

Scalp

Sebaceous Gland
Shaft of Hair
Sweat Duct
Arrector Pilli Muscle
Merocrine Sweat Gland
Hair Follicle
Matrix
Papilla

Epidermis
Dermis
Hypodermis

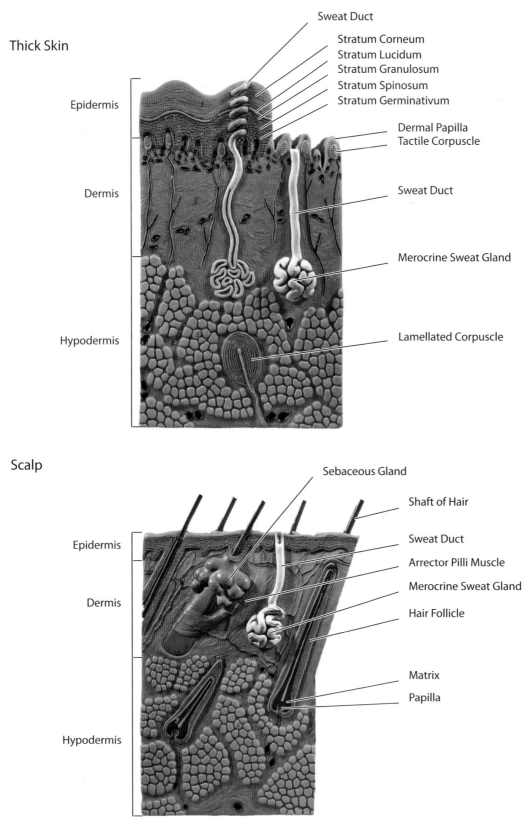

Thick Skin and Thin Skin - Histology

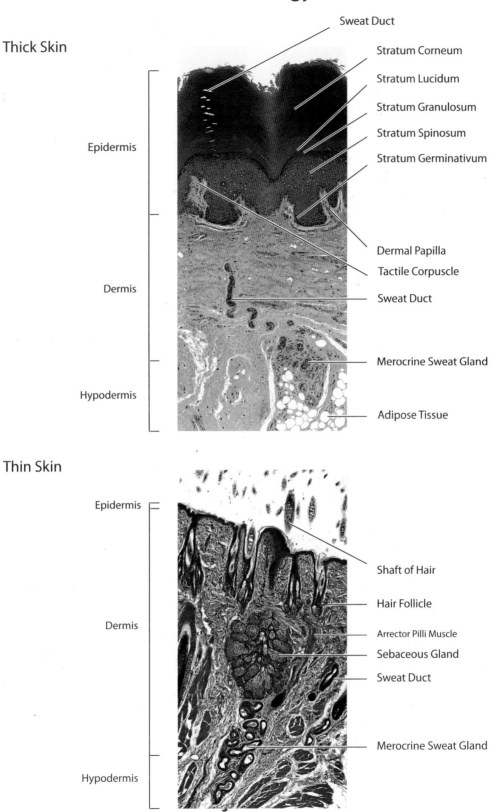

Thick Skin

Sweat Duct

Stratum Corneum

Stratum Lucidum

Stratum Granulosum

Stratum Spinosum

Stratum Germinativum

Epidermis

Dermal Papilla

Tactile Corpuscle

Dermis

Sweat Duct

Merocrine Sweat Gland

Hypodermis

Adipose Tissue

Thin Skin

Epidermis

Shaft of Hair

Hair Follicle

Dermis

Arrector Pilli Muscle

Sebaceous Gland

Sweat Duct

Merocrine Sweat Gland

Hypodermis

Scalp - Histology

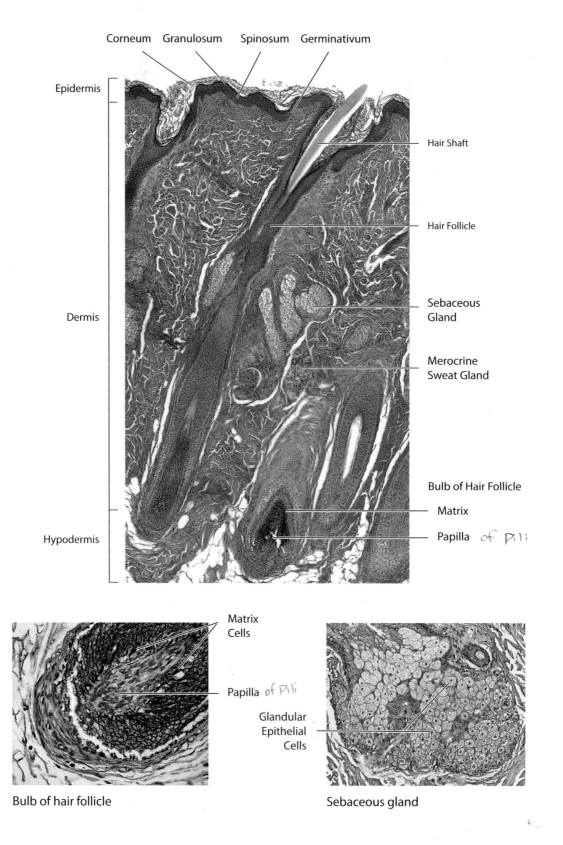

Corneum Granulosum Spinosum Germinativum

Epidermis

Hair Shaft

Hair Follicle

Dermis

Sebaceous
Gland

Merocrine
Sweat Gland

Bulb of Hair Follicle

Matrix

Hypodermis

Papilla of Pili

Matrix
Cells

Papilla of Pili

Glandular
Epithelial
Cells

Bulb of hair follicle

Sebaceous gland

Section 1 • Cells, Epithelial and Connective Tissues and Skin

Thick Skin - Histology

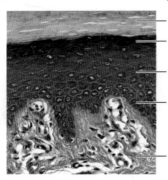

Stratum

Lucidum

Granulosum

Spinosum

Germinativum

Dermal papilla

Epidermis and Dermal papilla

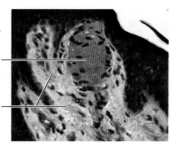

Tactile Receptor

Dermal Papilla

Tactile receptor in dermal papilla

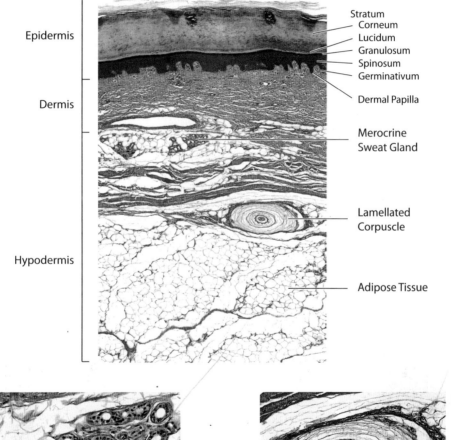

Epidermis

Dermis

Hypodermis

Stratum
Corneum
Lucidum
Granulosum
Spinosum
Germinativum

Dermal Papilla

Merocrine Sweat Gland

Lamellated Corpuscle

Adipose Tissue

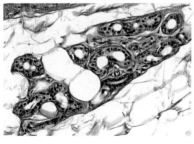

Merocrine sweat gland

Lamellated corpuscle

Section 2

Osseous Tissues, Bone and the Skeleton

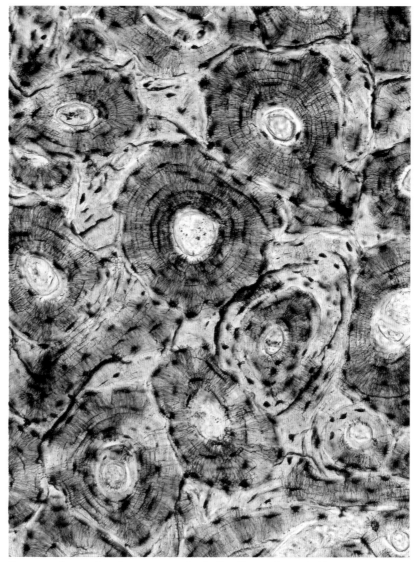

Compact bone showing osteons in shaft of bone (brightfield, x430)

Bone

Long Bone

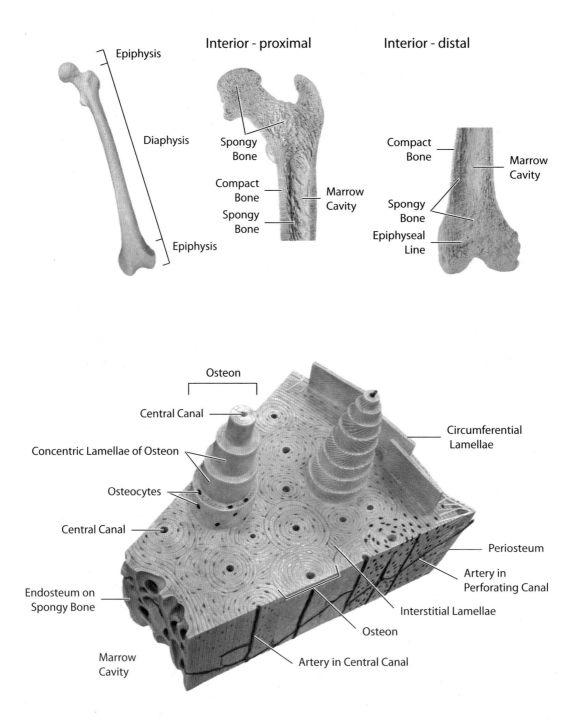

Epiphysis

Diaphysis

Epiphysis

Interior - proximal

Spongy Bone

Compact Bone

Spongy Bone

Marrow Cavity

Interior - distal

Compact Bone

Marrow Cavity

Spongy Bone

Epiphyseal Line

Osteon

Central Canal

Concentric Lamellae of Osteon

Osteocytes

Central Canal

Endosteum on Spongy Bone

Marrow Cavity

Circumferential Lamellae

Periosteum

Artery in Perforating Canal

Interstitial Lamellae

Osteon

Artery in Central Canal

Compact and Spongy Bone with Histology

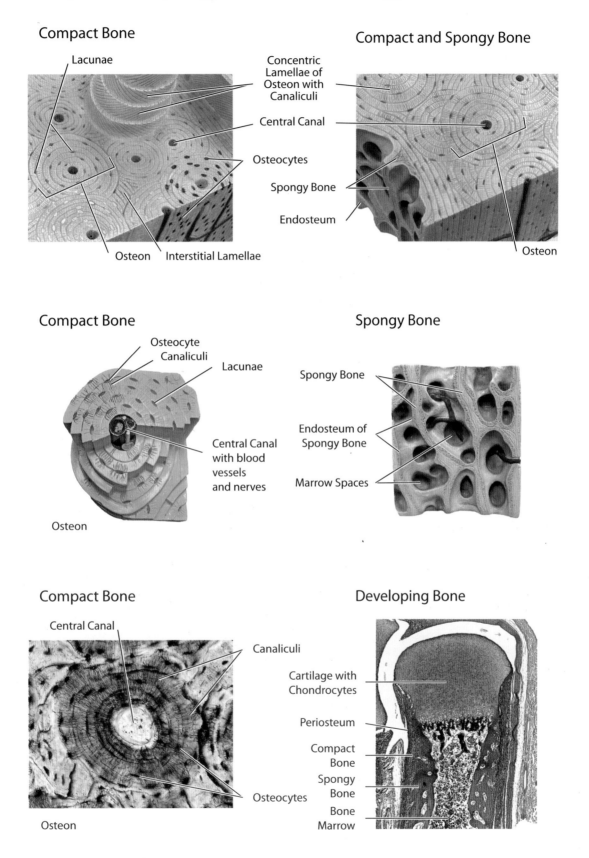

Compact Bone

Lacunae

Concentric Lamellae of Osteon with Canaliculi

Central Canal

Osteocytes

Osteon   Interstitial Lamellae

Compact and Spongy Bone

Spongy Bone

Endosteum

Osteon

Compact Bone

Osteocyte

Canaliculi

Lacunae

Central Canal with blood vessels and nerves

Osteon

Spongy Bone

Spongy Bone

Endosteum of Spongy Bone

Marrow Spaces

Compact Bone

Central Canal

Canaliculi

Osteocytes

Osteon

Developing Bone

Cartilage with Chondrocytes

Periosteum

Compact Bone

Spongy Bone

Bone Marrow

Epiphysis and Spongy Bone - Histology

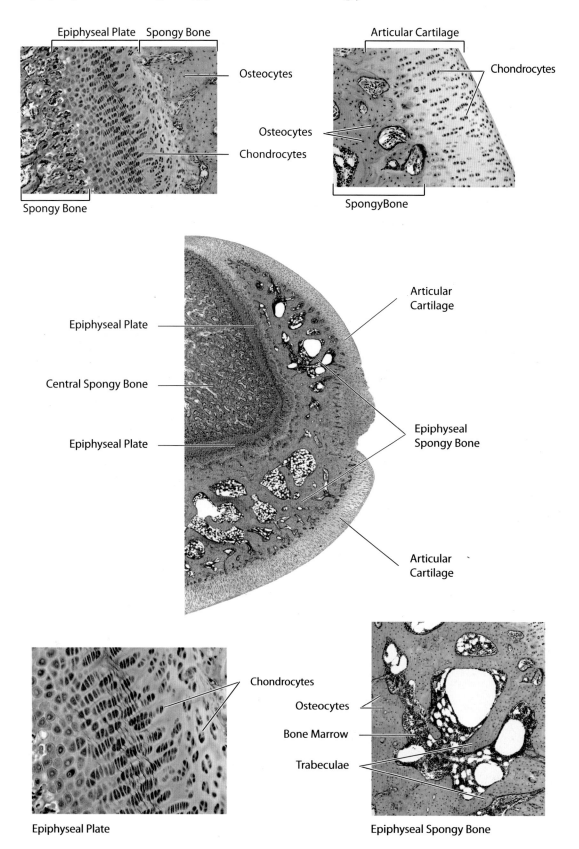

Epiphyseal Plate   Spongy Bone

Osteocytes

Osteocytes

Chondrocytes

Spongy Bone

Articular Cartilage

Chondrocytes

Osteocytes

Chondrocytes

SpongyBone

Epiphyseal Plate

Central Spongy Bone

Epiphyseal Plate

Articular Cartilage

Epiphyseal Spongy Bone

Articular Cartilage

Chondrocytes

Osteocytes

Bone Marrow

Trabeculae

Epiphyseal Plate

Epiphyseal Spongy Bone

Spongy Bone - Histology

Central Spongy Bone

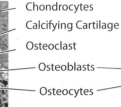

Chondrocytes
Calcifying Cartilage
Osteoclast
Osteoblasts
Osteocytes
Trabeculae

Epiphyseal Spongy Bone

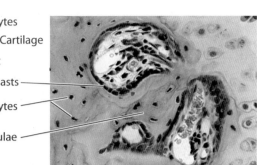

Osteoblasts
Osteocytes

Central Spongy Bone

Epiphyseal Spongy Bone

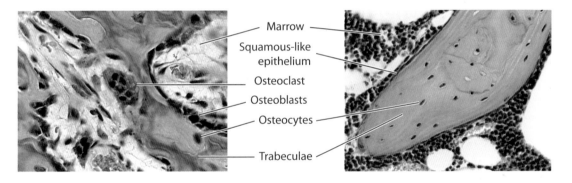

Marrow
Squamous-like epithelium
Osteoclast
Osteoblasts
Osteocytes
Trabeculae

Central Spongy Bone

Epiphyseal Spongy Bone

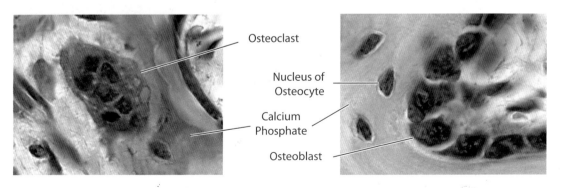

Osteoclast
Nucleus of Osteocyte
Calcium Phosphate
Osteoblast

Skull

Skull - Anterior

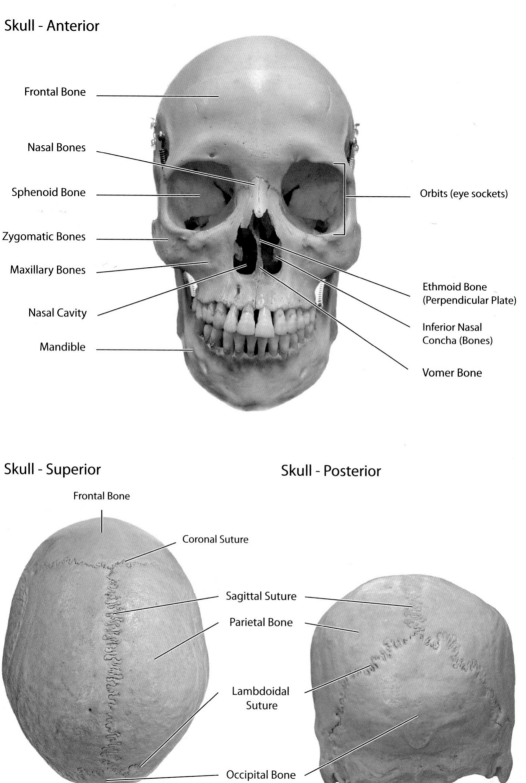

Frontal Bone

Nasal Bones

Sphenoid Bone

Zygomatic Bones

Maxillary Bones

Nasal Cavity

Mandible

Orbits (eye sockets)

Ethmoid Bone
(Perpendicular Plate)

Inferior Nasal
Concha (Bones)

Vomer Bone

Skull - Superior

Frontal Bone

Coronal Suture

Sagittal Suture

Parietal Bone

Lambdoidal
Suture

Occipital Bone

Skull - Posterior

Skull

Skull - Inferior

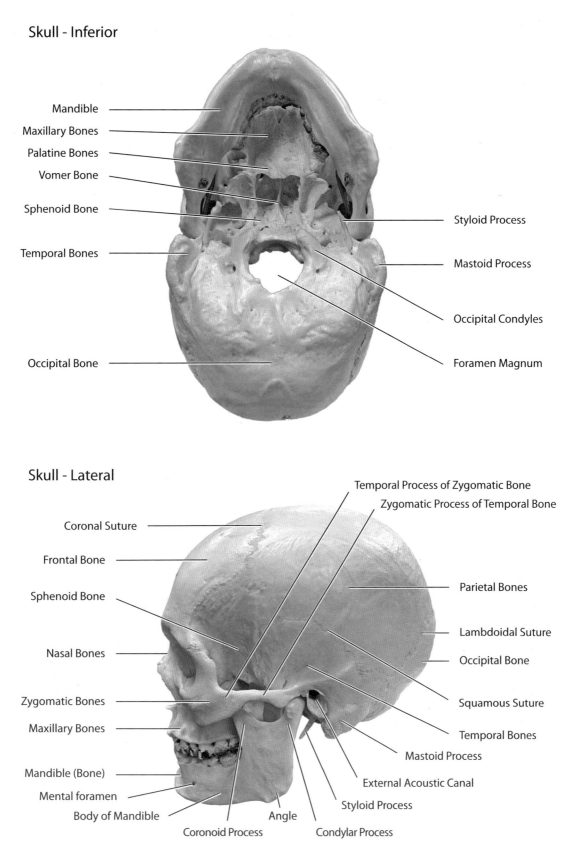

Mandible

Maxillary Bones

Palatine Bones

Vomer Bone

Sphenoid Bone

Temporal Bones

Occipital Bone

Styloid Process

Mastoid Process

Occipital Condyles

Foramen Magnum

Skull - Lateral

Temporal Process of Zygomatic Bone

Zygomatic Process of Temporal Bone

Coronal Suture

Frontal Bone

Sphenoid Bone

Nasal Bones

Zygomatic Bones

Maxillary Bones

Mandible (Bone)

Mental foramen

Body of Mandible

Coronoid Process

Angle

Styloid Process

Condylar Process

External Acoustic Canal

Mastoid Process

Temporal Bones

Squamous Suture

Occipital Bone

Lambdoidal Suture

Parietal Bones

Skull

Skull - Midsagittal

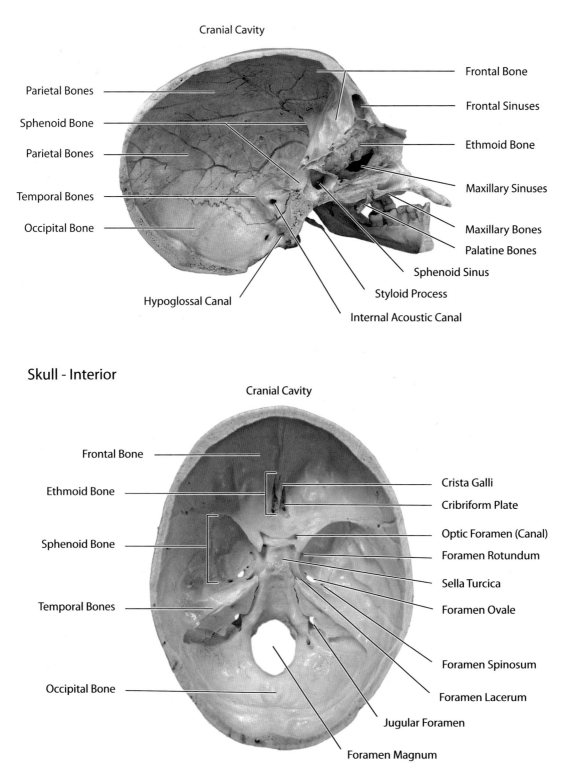

Cranial Cavity

Parietal Bones

Sphenoid Bone

Parietal Bones

Temporal Bones

Occipital Bone

Frontal Bone

Frontal Sinuses

Ethmoid Bone

Maxillary Sinuses

Maxillary Bones

Palatine Bones

Sphenoid Sinus

Styloid Process

Internal Acoustic Canal

Hypoglossal Canal

Skull - Interior

Cranial Cavity

Frontal Bone

Ethmoid Bone

Sphenoid Bone

Temporal Bones

Occipital Bone

Crista Galli

Cribriform Plate

Optic Foramen (Canal)

Foramen Rotundum

Sella Turcica

Foramen Ovale

Foramen Spinosum

Foramen Lacerum

Jugular Foramen

Foramen Magnum

Skull

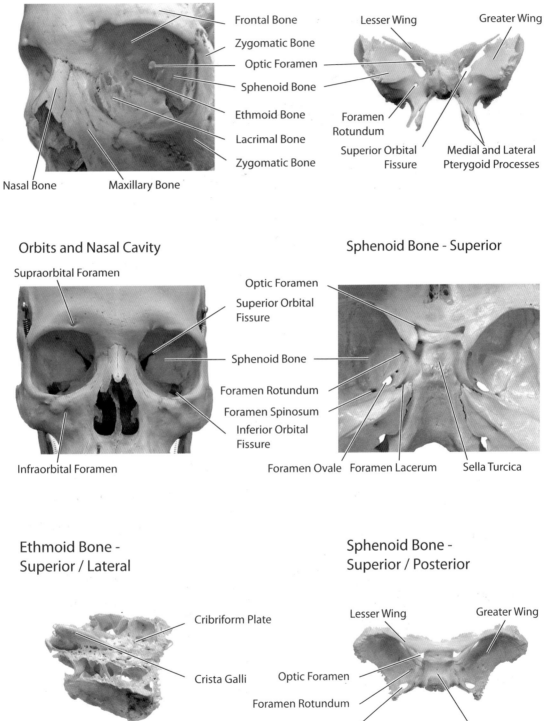

Orbit

Frontal Bone
Zygomatic Bone
Optic Foramen
Sphenoid Bone
Ethmoid Bone
Lacrimal Bone
Zygomatic Bone
Nasal Bone
Maxillary Bone

Sphenoid Bone - Anterior

Lesser Wing
Greater Wing
Foramen Rotundum
Superior Orbital Fissure
Medial and Lateral Pterygoid Processes

Orbits and Nasal Cavity

Supraorbital Foramen
Superior Orbital Fissure
Sphenoid Bone
Foramen Rotundum
Foramen Spinosum
Inferior Orbital Fissure
Infraorbital Foramen

Sphenoid Bone - Superior

Optic Foramen
Foramen Ovale
Foramen Lacerum
Sella Turcica

Ethmoid Bone - Superior / Lateral

Cribriform Plate
Crista Galli

Sphenoid Bone - Superior / Posterior

Lesser Wing
Greater Wing
Optic Foramen
Foramen Rotundum
Foramen Ovale
Sella Turcica

Skull

Temporal Bone - Lateral

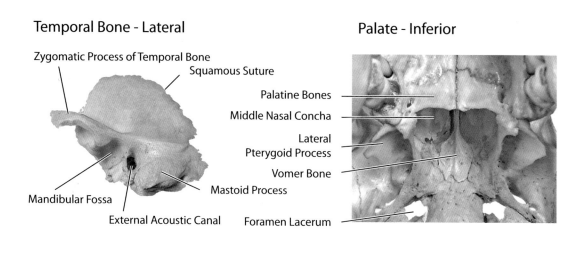

Zygomatic Process of Temporal Bone
Squamous Suture
Mandibular Fossa
Mastoid Process
External Acoustic Canal

Palate - Inferior

Palatine Bones
Middle Nasal Concha
Lateral Pterygoid Process
Vomer Bone
Foramen Lacerum

Temporal Bone - Inferior

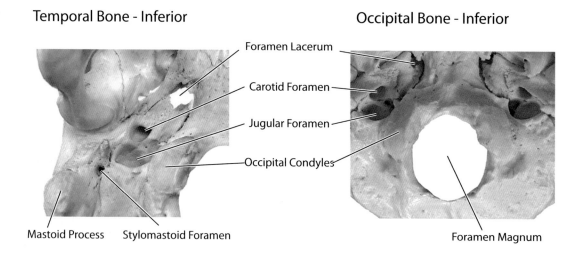

Foramen Lacerum
Carotid Foramen
Jugular Foramen
Occipital Condyles
Mastoid Process
Stylomastoid Foramen

Occipital Bone - Inferior

Occipital Condyles
Foramen Magnum

Temporal Bone - Medial

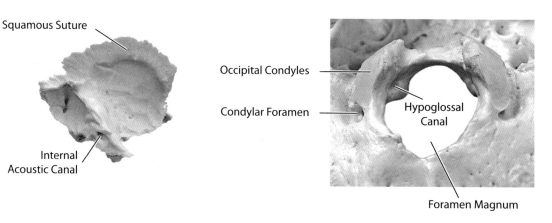

Squamous Suture
Internal Acoustic Canal

Occipital Bone - Inferior

Occipital Condyles
Condylar Foramen
Hypoglossal Canal
Foramen Magnum

Vertebrae

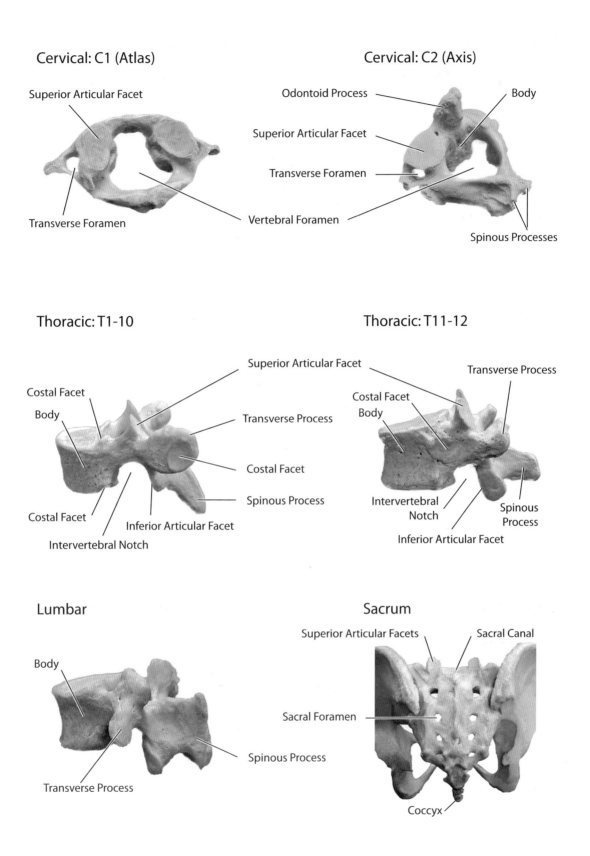

Cervical: C1 (Atlas)

Superior Articular Facet

Transverse Foramen

Cervical: C2 (Axis)

Odontoid Process

Body

Superior Articular Facet

Transverse Foramen

Vertebral Foramen

Spinous Processes

Thoracic: T1-10

Costal Facet

Body

Superior Articular Facet

Transverse Process

Costal Facet

Spinous Process

Costal Facet

Inferior Articular Facet

Intervertebral Notch

Thoracic: T11-12

Superior Articular Facet

Transverse Process

Costal Facet

Body

Intervertebral Notch

Spinous Process

Inferior Articular Facet

Lumbar

Body

Transverse Process

Spinous Process

Sacrum

Superior Articular Facets

Sacral Canal

Sacral Foramen

Coccyx

Ribs, Vertebrae, and Sternum

Ribs

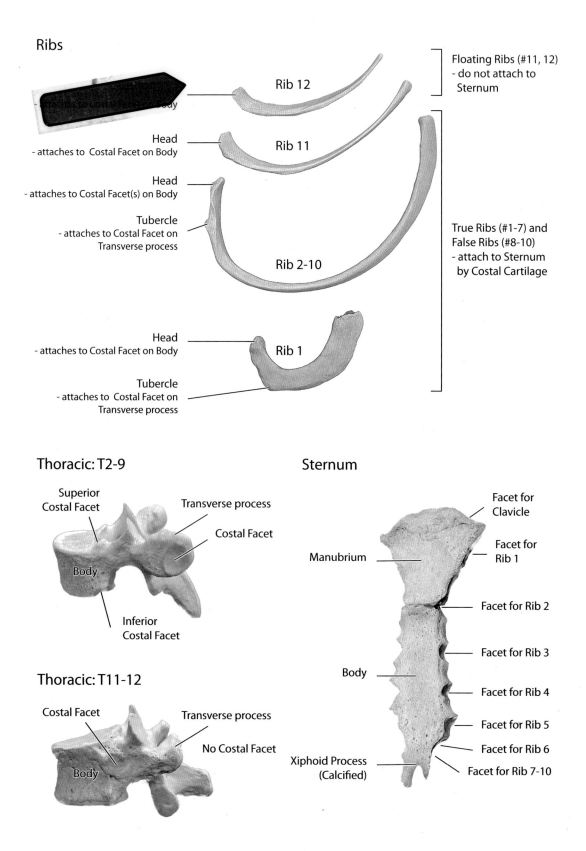

Rib 12

Floating Ribs (#11, 12)
- do not attach to Sternum

Head
- attaches to Costal Facet on Body

Rib 11

Head
- attaches to Costal Facet(s) on Body

Tubercle
- attaches to Costal Facet on Transverse process

Rib 2-10

True Ribs (#1-7) and False Ribs (#8-10)
- attach to Sternum by Costal Cartilage

Head
- attaches to Costal Facet on Body

Rib 1

Tubercle
- attaches to Costal Facet on Transverse process

Thoracic: T2-9

Superior Costal Facet

Transverse process

Costal Facet

Body

Inferior Costal Facet

Thoracic: T11-12

Costal Facet

Transverse process

No Costal Facet

Body

Sternum

Facet for Clavicle

Facet for Rib 1

Manubrium

Facet for Rib 2

Facet for Rib 3

Body

Facet for Rib 4

Facet for Rib 5

Facet for Rib 6

Xiphoid Process (Calcified)

Facet for Rib 7-10

Scapula

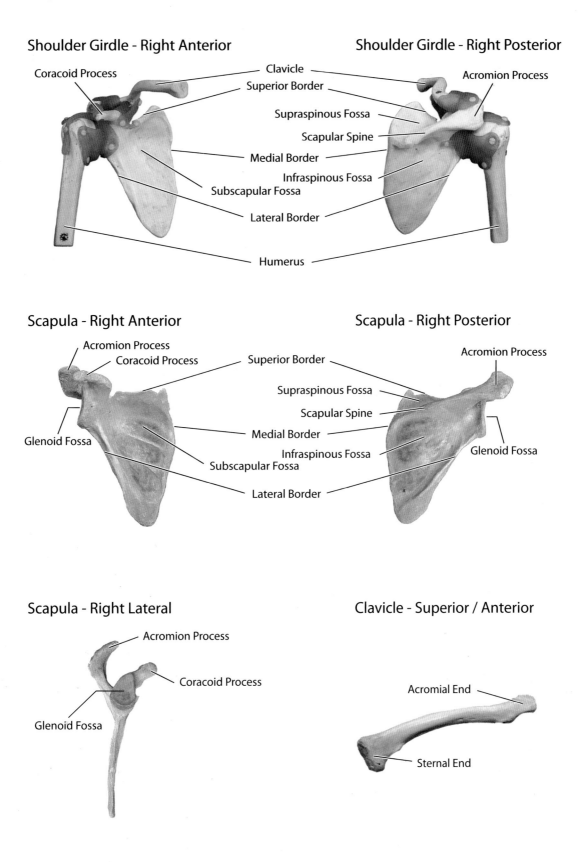

Shoulder Girdle - Right Anterior

Coracoid Process
Clavicle
Superior Border
Supraspinous Fossa
Scapular Spine
Medial Border
Infraspinous Fossa
Subscapular Fossa
Lateral Border
Humerus

Shoulder Girdle - Right Posterior

Acromion Process

Scapula - Right Anterior

Acromion Process
Coracoid Process
Superior Border
Supraspinous Fossa
Scapular Spine
Medial Border
Infraspinous Fossa
Subscapular Fossa
Lateral Border
Glenoid Fossa

Scapula - Right Posterior

Acromion Process
Glenoid Fossa

Scapula - Right Lateral

Acromion Process
Coracoid Process
Glenoid Fossa

Clavicle - Superior / Anterior

Acromial End
Sternal End

Humerus

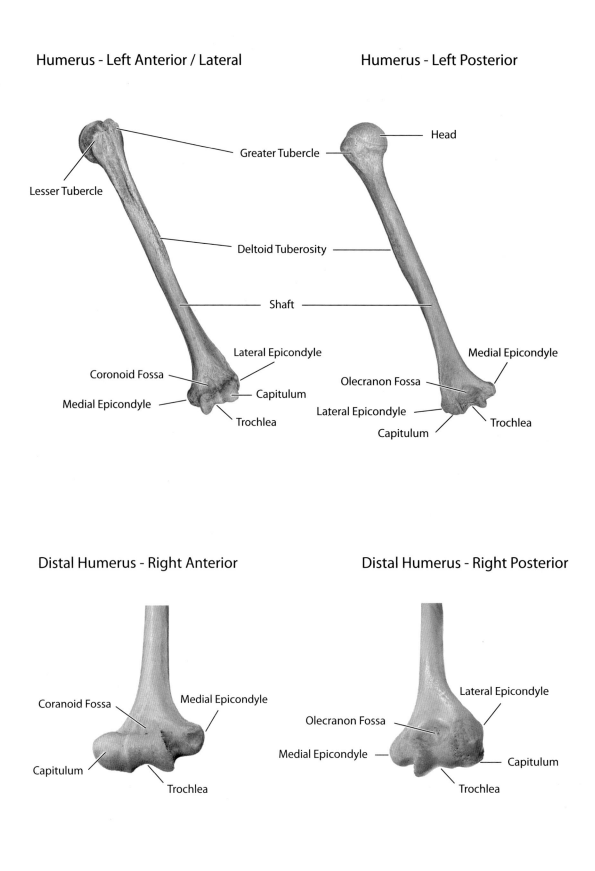

Humerus - Left Anterior / Lateral

Greater Tubercle

Lesser Tubercle

Deltoid Tuberosity

Shaft

Lateral Epicondyle

Coronoid Fossa

Medial Epicondyle

Capitulum

Trochlea

Humerus - Left Posterior

Head

Deltoid Tuberosity

Medial Epicondyle

Olecranon Fossa

Lateral Epicondyle

Capitulum

Trochlea

Distal Humerus - Right Anterior

Coranoid Fossa

Medial Epicondyle

Capitulum

Trochlea

Distal Humerus - Right Posterior

Lateral Epicondyle

Olecranon Fossa

Medial Epicondyle

Capitulum

Trochlea

Ulna and Radius

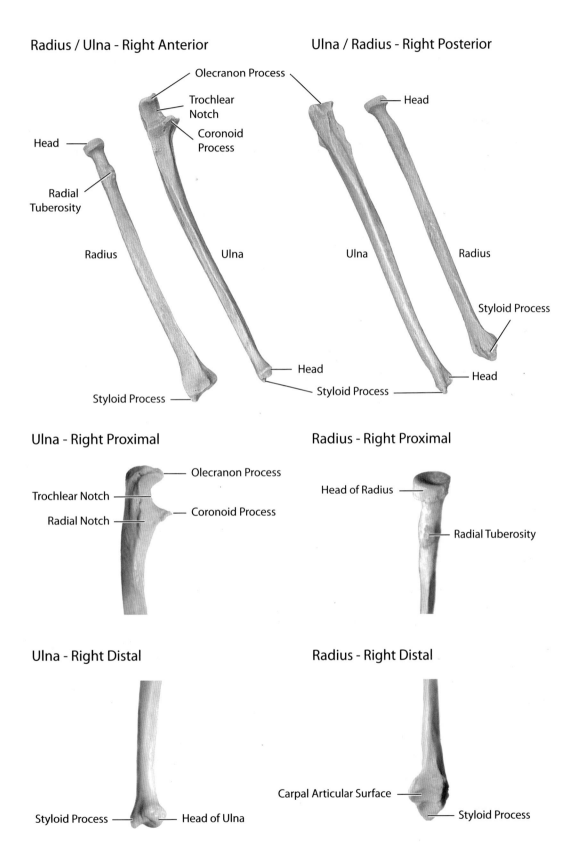

Radius / Ulna - Right Anterior

Olecranon Process

Trochlear Notch

Coronoid Process

Head

Radial Tuberosity

Radius

Ulna

Styloid Process

Head

Styloid Process

Ulna / Radius - Right Posterior

Head

Ulna

Radius

Styloid Process

Head

Ulna - Right Proximal

Olecranon Process

Trochlear Notch

Coronoid Process

Radial Notch

Radius - Right Proximal

Head of Radius

Radial Tuberosity

Ulna - Right Distal

Styloid Process

Head of Ulna

Radius - Right Distal

Carpal Articular Surface

Styloid Process

Hand

Hand - Right Anterior

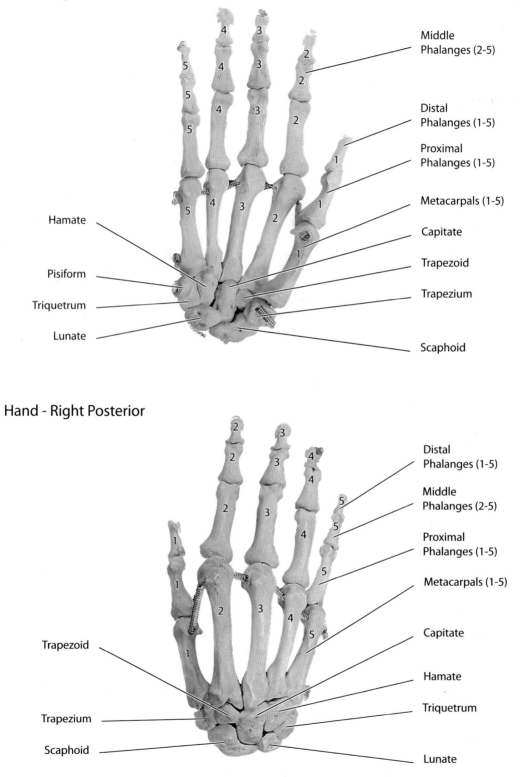

Middle
Phalanges (2-5)

Distal
Phalanges (1-5)

Proximal
Phalanges (1-5)

Metacarpals (1-5)

Capitate

Trapezoid

Trapezium

Scaphoid

Hamate

Pisiform

Triquetrum

Lunate

Hand - Right Posterior

Distal
Phalanges (1-5)

Middle
Phalanges (2-5)

Proximal
Phalanges (1-5)

Metacarpals (1-5)

Capitate

Hamate

Triquetrum

Lunate

Trapezoid

Trapezium

Scaphoid

Pelvic Girdle

Coxa - Right Medial

Iliac Crest

Anterior Superior
Iliac Spine

Anterior Inferior
Iliac Spine

Sacral Articular Surface

Posterior Superior
Iliac Spine

Posterior Inferior
Iliac Spine

Greater Sciatic Notch

Ischial Spine

Superior Ramus of Pubis

Lesser Sciatic Notch

Pubic Body

Obturator Foramen

Pubic Symphysis

Ischial Ramus
Inferior Ramus of Pubis

Coxae - Posterior

Posterior Superior
Iliac Spines

Sacrum

Ischial Tuberosity

Coxa - Right Posterior / Lateral

Iliac Crest

Posterior Superior
Iliac Spine

Coxa - R Lateral

Ilium

Posterior Inferior
Iliac Spine

Greater Sciatic Notch

Anterior Superior
Iliac Spine

Anterior Inferior
Iliac Spine

Acetabulum

Ischial Spine

Acetabulum

Lesser Sciatic Notch

Inferior Ramus of Pubis

Ischial Tuberosity

Ischial Ramus

Ischial Tuberosity

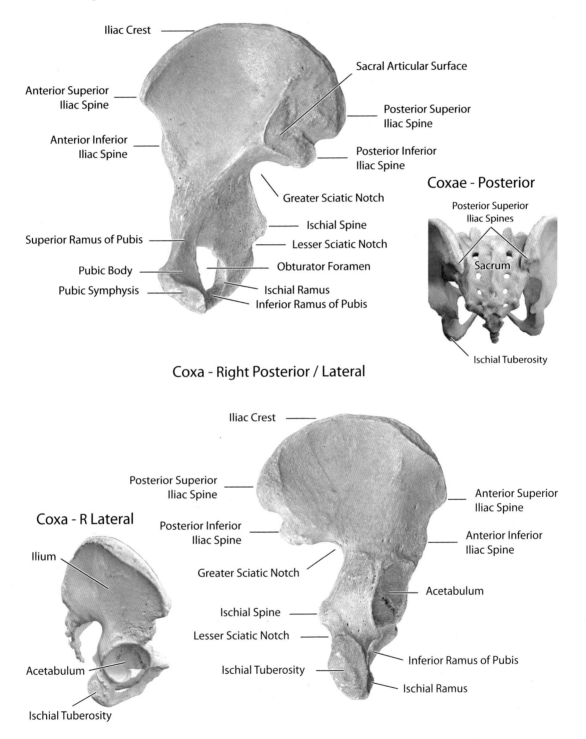

Femur

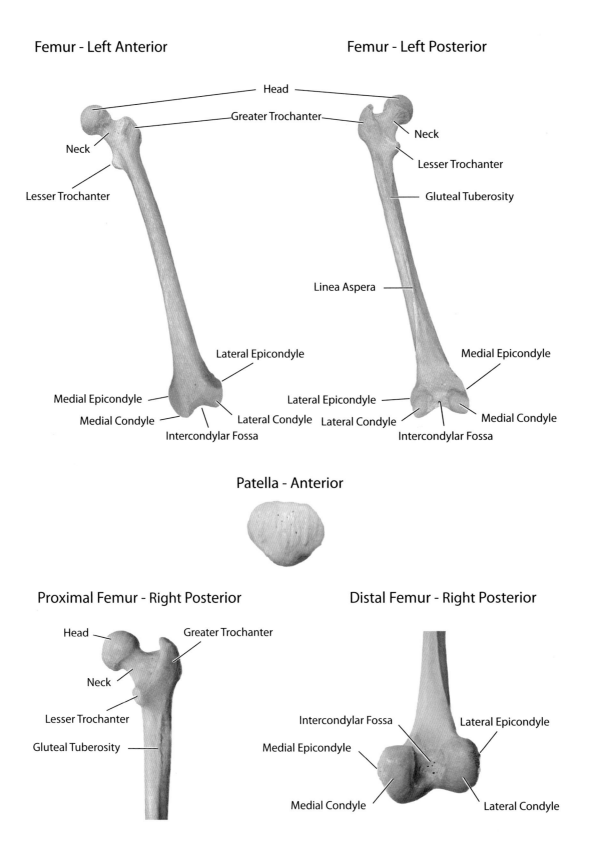

Femur - Left Anterior

- Head
- Greater Trochanter
- Neck
- Lesser Trochanter
- Lateral Epicondyle
- Medial Epicondyle
- Medial Condyle
- Intercondylar Fossa
- Lateral Condyle

Femur - Left Posterior

- Head
- Greater Trochanter
- Neck
- Lesser Trochanter
- Gluteal Tuberosity
- Linea Aspera
- Medial Epicondyle
- Lateral Epicondyle
- Lateral Condyle
- Intercondylar Fossa
- Medial Condyle

Patella - Anterior

Proximal Femur - Right Posterior

- Head
- Greater Trochanter
- Neck
- Lesser Trochanter
- Gluteal Tuberosity

Distal Femur - Right Posterior

- Intercondylar Fossa
- Medial Epicondyle
- Lateral Epicondyle
- Medial Condyle
- Lateral Condyle

Tibia

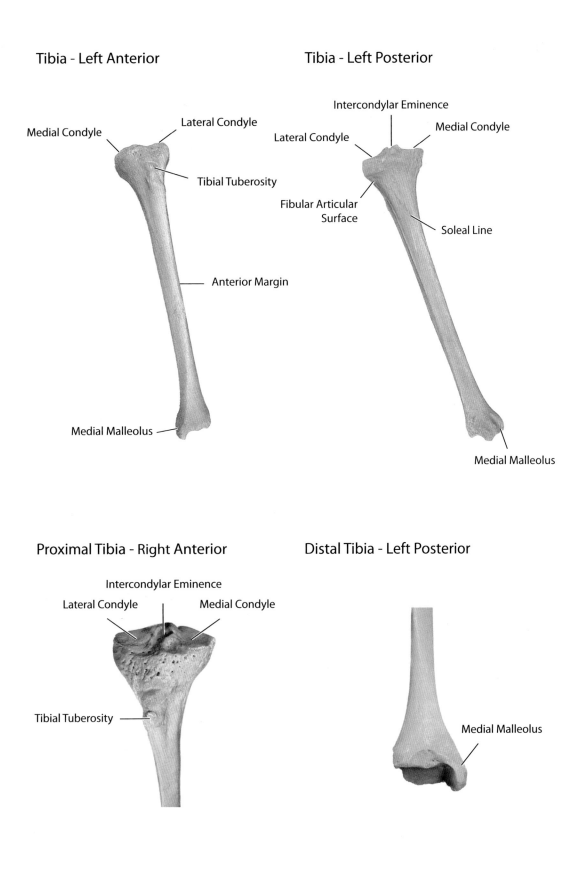

Tibia - Left Anterior

Medial Condyle
Lateral Condyle
Tibial Tuberosity
Anterior Margin
Medial Malleolus

Tibia - Left Posterior

Intercondylar Eminence
Medial Condyle
Lateral Condyle
Fibular Articular Surface
Soleal Line
Medial Malleolus

Proximal Tibia - Right Anterior

Intercondylar Eminence
Lateral Condyle
Medial Condyle
Tibial Tuberosity

Distal Tibia - Left Posterior

Medial Malleolus

Fibula and Foot

Fibula - Left Anterior

Fibula - Left Posterior

Distal Fibula - Left Anterior

Foot - Right Superior

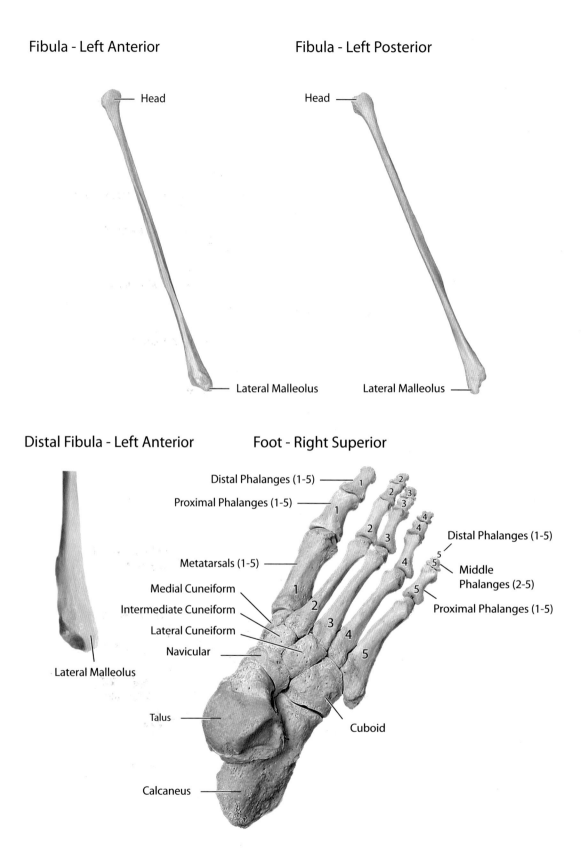

Head

Head

Lateral Malleolus

Lateral Malleolus

Distal Phalanges (1-5)

Proximal Phalanges (1-5)

Distal Phalanges (1-5)

Middle Phalanges (2-5)

Proximal Phalanges (1-5)

Metatarsals (1-5)

Medial Cuneiform

Intermediate Cuneiform

Lateral Cuneiform

Navicular

Lateral Malleolus

Talus

Cuboid

Calcaneus

Knee Joint

Knee - Right Anterior

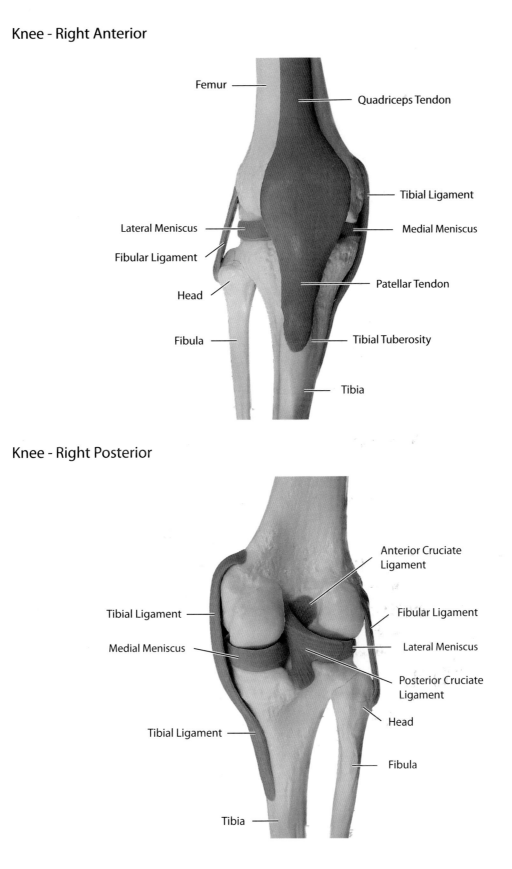

Femur

Quadriceps Tendon

Tibial Ligament

Lateral Meniscus

Medial Meniscus

Fibular Ligament

Head

Patellar Tendon

Fibula

Tibial Tuberosity

Tibia

Knee - Right Posterior

Anterior Cruciate
Ligament

Tibial Ligament

Fibular Ligament

Medial Meniscus

Lateral Meniscus

Posterior Cruciate
Ligament

Head

Tibial Ligament

Fibula

Tibia

Section 3

Muscle Tissues
and Skeletal Muscles

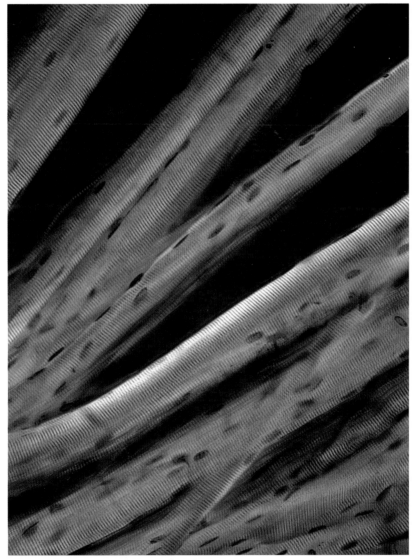

Skeletal muscle cells showing banding (polarized light, lambda; x300)

Skeletal Muscle and Cells

Shoulder Muscles - Anterior

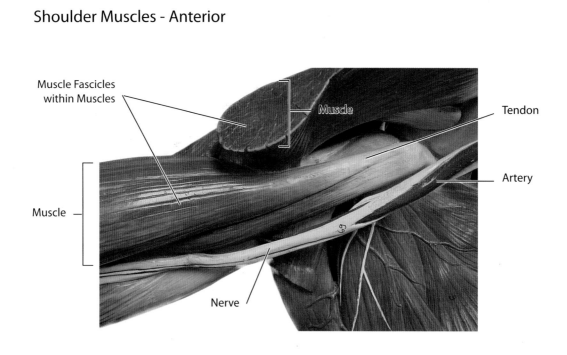

Muscle Fascicles within Muscles

Muscle

Muscle

Tendon

Artery

Muscle

Nerve

Telephone Cable as Skeletal Muscle

Skeletal Muscle Cell

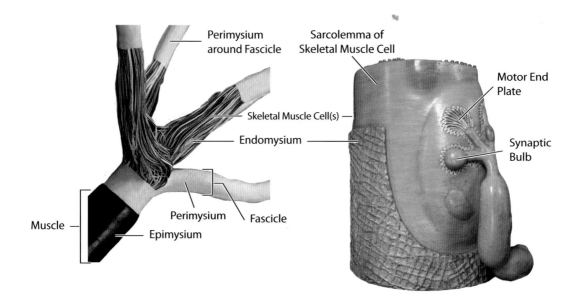

Perimysium around Fascicle

Skeletal Muscle Cell(s)

Endomysium

Muscle

Perimysium

Fascicle

Epimysium

Sarcolemma of Skeletal Muscle Cell

Motor End Plate

Synaptic Bulb

Skeletal Muscle Cell

Skeletal Muscle Cell
- longitudinal section

Skeletal Muscle Cell
- cross section

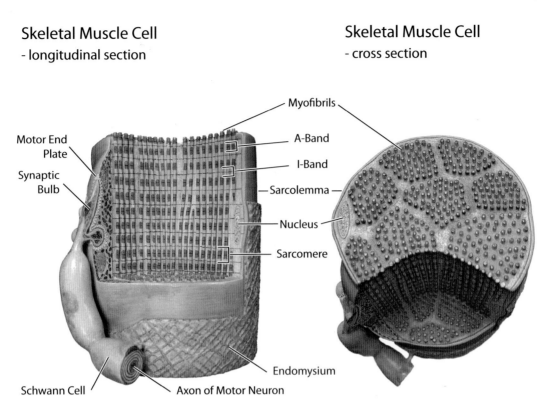

Myofibrils

A-Band

I-Band

Sarcolemma

Nucleus

Sarcomere

Motor End Plate

Synaptic Bulb

Endomysium

Schwann Cell

Axon of Motor Neuron

Sarcomere and Sarcoplasmic Reticulum

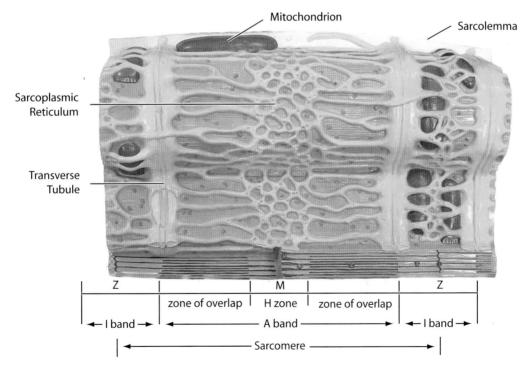

Mitochondrion

Sarcolemma

Sarcoplasmic Reticulum

Transverse Tubule

Z

M

Z

zone of overlap   H zone   zone of overlap

← I band →   ← A band →   ← I band →

← Sarcomere →

Skeletal Muscle Tissue - Histology

Nerve and Muscle
- longitudinal section (vertical)

Skeletal
Muscle Cells

Synaptic
Bulbs

Skeletal Muscle Cells
- longitudinal section (horizontal)

Skeletal
Muscle Cells

A-Band

I-Band
with Z-line

Skeletal Muscle Fascicles and Cells
- cross section

Perimysium

Skeletal
Muscle Cells

Endomysium

Fascicle

Skeletal Muscle Cells

Skeletal Muscle Cells
- longitudinal section

Skeletal
Muscle Cells

Skeletal Muscle Cells and Myofibrils
- cross section

Perimysium

Myofibrils
within
Skeletal
Muscle Cells

Skeletal Muscle Cells
- longitudinal section

A-Band

I-Band

Sarcomere (Z-line to Z-line)

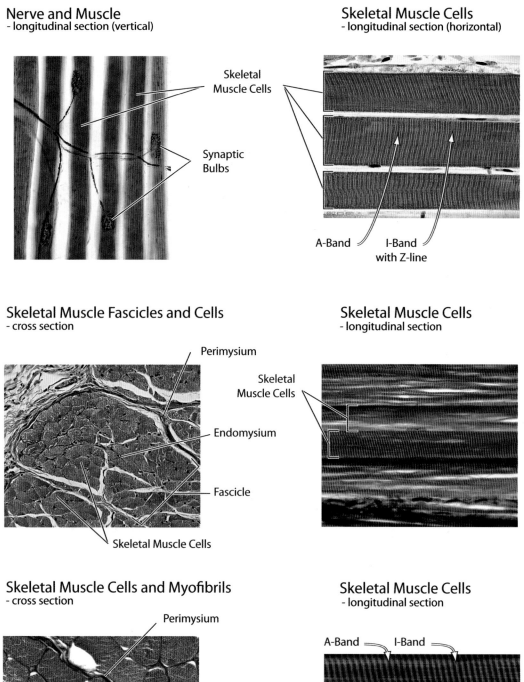

Muscles of the Head and Neck

Head Muscles - Anterior

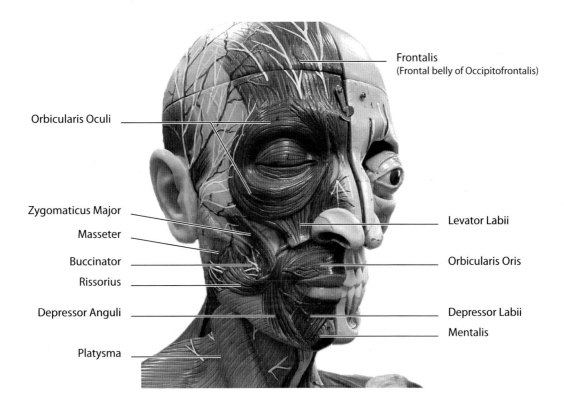

Frontalis
(Frontal belly of Occipitofrontalis)

Orbicularis Oculi

Zygomaticus Major

Masseter

Buccinator

Rissorius

Depressor Anguli

Platysma

Levator Labii

Orbicularis Oris

Depressor Labii

Mentalis

Head Muscles - Posterior

Head Muscles - Lateral

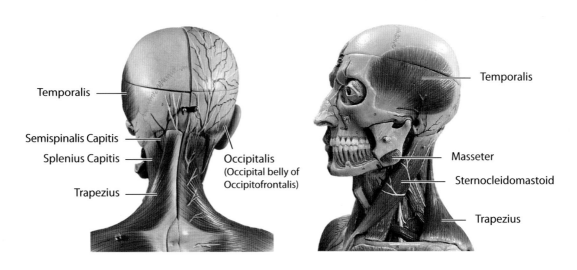

Temporalis

Semispinalis Capitis

Splenius Capitis

Trapezius

Occipitalis
(Occipital belly of
Occipitofrontalis)

Temporalis

Masseter

Sternocleidomastoid

Trapezius

Muscles of the Head and Neck

Neck Muscles - Lateral

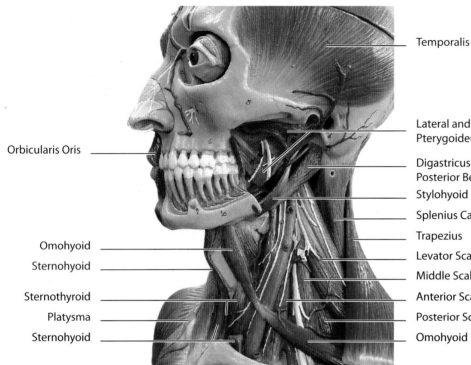

Temporalis

Lateral and Medial Pterygoideus

Digastricus - Posterior Belly

Stylohyoid

Splenius Capitis

Trapezius

Levator Scapula

Middle Scalene

Anterior Scalene

Posterior Scalene

Omohyoid

Orbicularis Oris

Omohyoid

Sternohyoid

Sternothyroid

Platysma

Sternohyoid

Neck Muscles - Lateral / Inferior

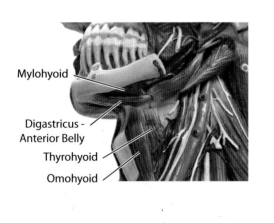

Mylohyoid

Digastricus - Anterior Belly

Thyrohyoid

Omohyoid

Neck Muscles - Midsagittal

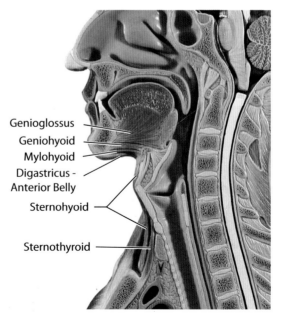

Genioglossus

Geniohyoid

Mylohyoid

Digastricus - Anterior Belly

Sternohyoid

Sternothyroid

Muscles of the Eye

Extrinsic Eye Muscles - Lateral

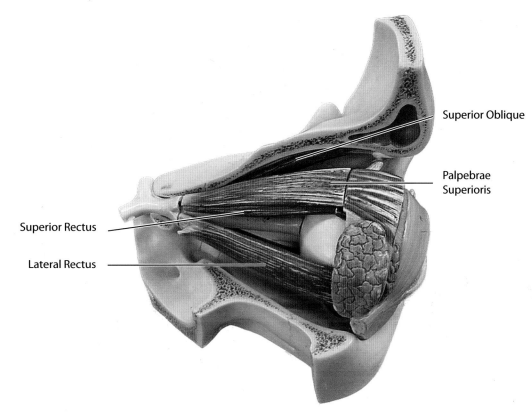

Superior Oblique

Palpebrae Superioris

Superior Rectus

Lateral Rectus

Extrinsic Eye Muscles - Superior   Extrinsic Eye Muscles - Posterior

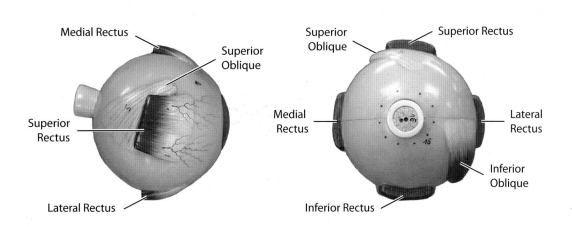

Medial Rectus

Superior Oblique

Superior Rectus

Lateral Rectus

Superior Oblique

Superior Rectus

Medial Rectus

Lateral Rectus

Inferior Oblique

Inferior Rectus

Muscles of the Neck, Back and Trunk

Trunk - Posterior

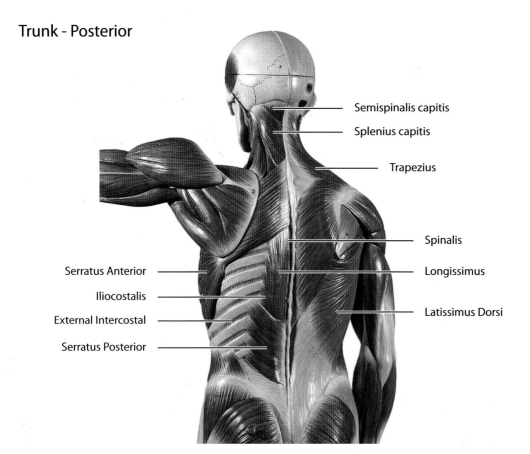

Semispinalis capitis

Splenius capitis

Trapezius

Spinalis

Serratus Anterior

Longissimus

Iliocostalis

External Intercostal

Latissimus Dorsi

Serratus Posterior

Head and Neck - Posterior

Temporalis

Semispinalis capitis

Semispinalis capitis

Splenius capitis

Sternocleidomastoid

Splenius capitis

Trapezius

Trapezius

Infraspinatus

Deltoid

Muscles of the Neck and Trunk

Neck - Lateral

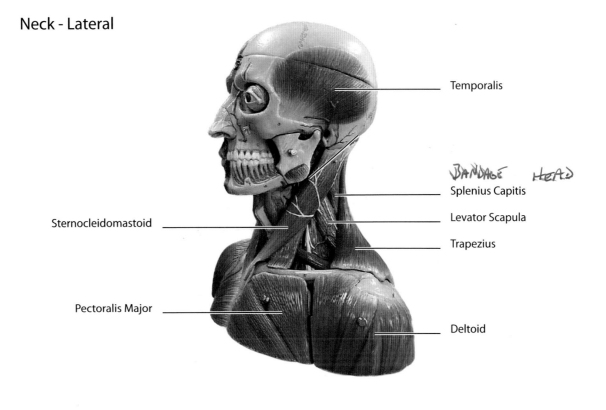

Temporalis

BANDAGE HEAD

Splenius Capitis

Sternocleidomastoid

Levator Scapula

Trapezius

Pectoralis Major

Deltoid

Neck - Lateral

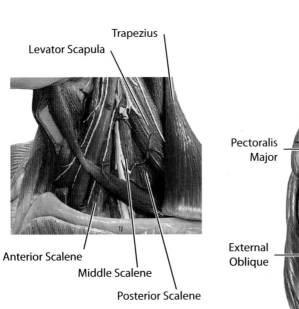

Trapezius

Levator Scapula

Anterior Scalene

Middle Scalene

Posterior Scalene

Trunk - Anterior

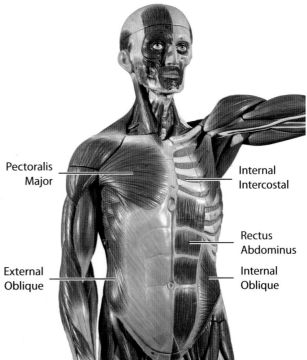

Pectoralis Major

Internal Intercostal

External Oblique

Rectus Abdominus

Internal Oblique

Muscles of the Trunk

Trunk - Anterior / Exterior

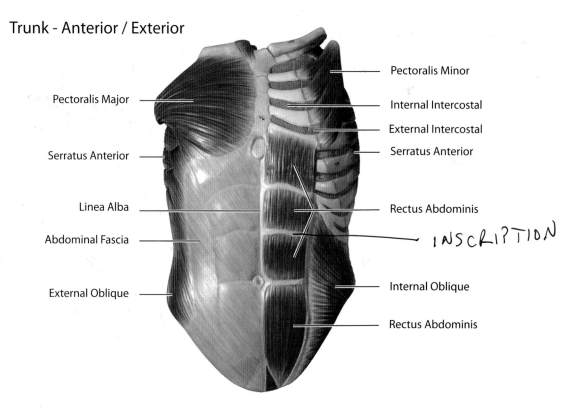

Pectoralis Major

Serratus Anterior

Linea Alba

Abdominal Fascia

External Oblique

Pectoralis Minor

Internal Intercostal

External Intercostal

Serratus Anterior

Rectus Abdominis

INSCRIPTION

Internal Oblique

Rectus Abdominis

Trunk - Anterior / Interior

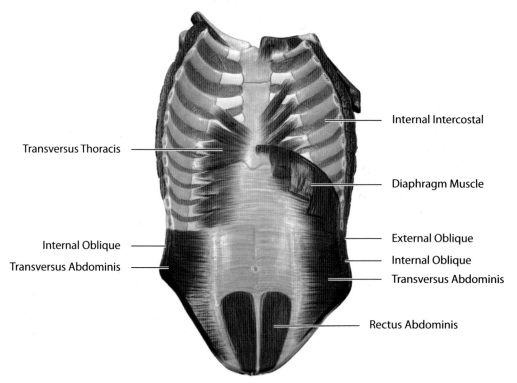

Transversus Thoracis

Internal Oblique

Transversus Abdominis

Internal Intercostal

Diaphragm Muscle

External Oblique

Internal Oblique

Transversus Abdominis

Rectus Abdominis

Muscles of the Shoulders and Arms

Trunk and Arms - Anterior

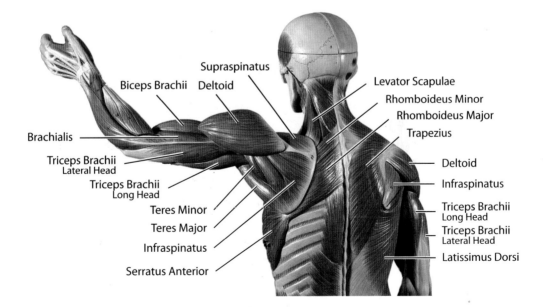

Deltoid

Biceps Brachii

Trapezius

Deltoid

Pectoralis Major

Triceps Brachii
Lateral Head

Brachialis

Biceps Brachii

Brachioradialis

Triceps Brachii
Medial Head

Triceps Brachii
Long Head

Coracobrachialis

Teres Major

Pectoralis Minor

Serratus Anterior

Trunk and Arms - Posterior

Supraspinatus

Biceps Brachii

Deltoid

Levator Scapulae

Rhomboideus Minor

Rhomboideus Major

Trapezius

Brachialis

Triceps Brachii
Lateral Head

Triceps Brachii
Long Head

Teres Minor

Teres Major

Infraspinatus

Serratus Anterior

Deltoid

Infraspinatus

Triceps Brachii
Long Head

Triceps Brachii
Lateral Head

Latissimus Dorsi

Muscles of the Arm

Arm - Anterior / medial

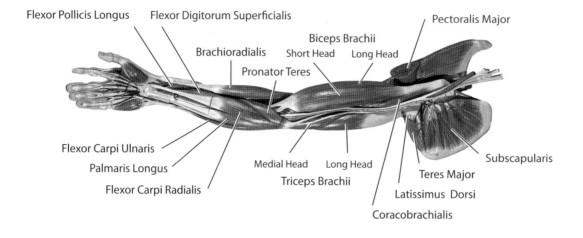

Flexor Pollicis Longus   Flexor Digitorum Superficialis   Pectoralis Major

Biceps Brachii

Brachioradialis   Short Head   Long Head

Pronator Teres

Flexor Carpi Ulnaris

Palmaris Longus

Flexor Carpi Radialis

Medial Head   Long Head

Triceps Brachii

Subscapularis

Teres Major

Latissimus Dorsi

Coracobrachialis

Arm - Posterior / Lateral

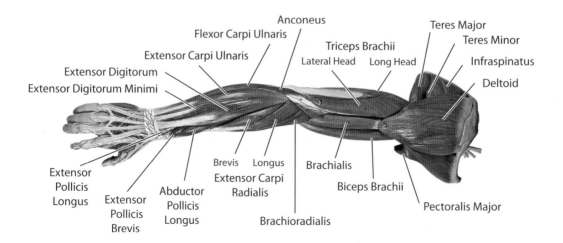

Anconeus

Flexor Carpi Ulnaris

Extensor Carpi Ulnaris

Triceps Brachii

Lateral Head   Long Head

Teres Major

Teres Minor

Infraspinatus

Extensor Digitorum

Extensor Digitorum Minimi

Deltoid

Extensor
Pollicis
Longus

Extensor
Pollicis
Brevis

Abductor
Pollicis
Longus

Brevis   Longus

Extensor Carpi
Radialis

Brachialis

Biceps Brachii

Pectoralis Major

Brachioradialis

Muscles of the Lower Arm

Lower Arm - Anterior / Medial

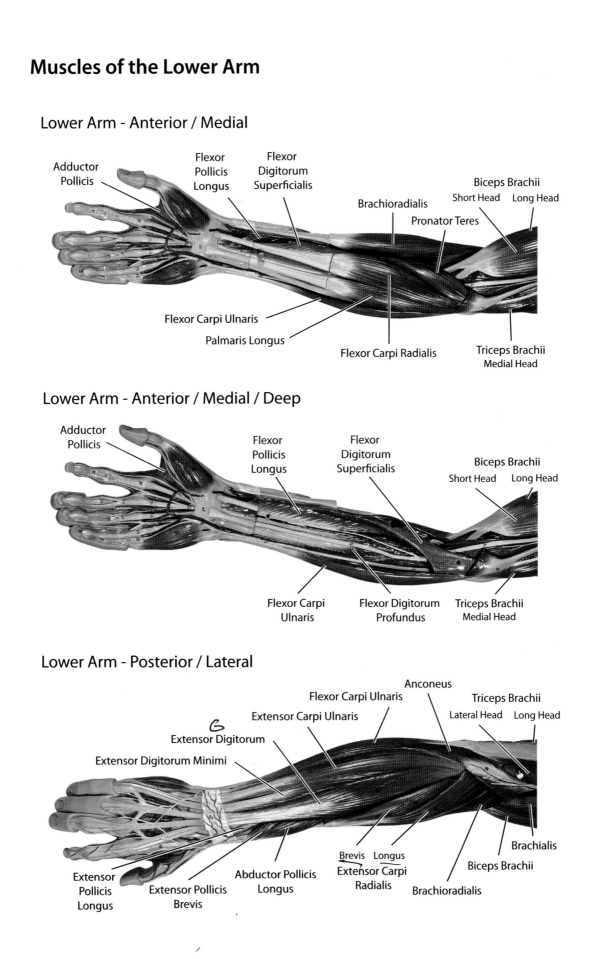

Adductor Pollicis

Flexor Pollicis Longus

Flexor Digitorum Superficialis

Brachioradialis

Pronator Teres

Biceps Brachii
Short Head — Long Head

Flexor Carpi Ulnaris

Palmaris Longus

Flexor Carpi Radialis

Triceps Brachii
Medial Head

Lower Arm - Anterior / Medial / Deep

Adductor Pollicis

Flexor Pollicis Longus

Flexor Digitorum Superficialis

Biceps Brachii
Short Head — Long Head

Flexor Carpi Ulnaris

Flexor Digitorum Profundus

Triceps Brachii
Medial Head

Lower Arm - Posterior / Lateral

Anconeus

Flexor Carpi Ulnaris

Extensor Carpi Ulnaris

Triceps Brachii
Lateral Head — Long Head

Extensor Digitorum

Extensor Digitorum Minimi

Extensor Pollicis Longus

Extensor Pollicis Brevis

Abductor Pollicis Longus

Brevis   Longus
Extensor Carpi Radialis

Brachialis

Biceps Brachii

Brachioradialis

Muscles of the Hip, Thighs and Legs

Thigh and Leg - Anterior

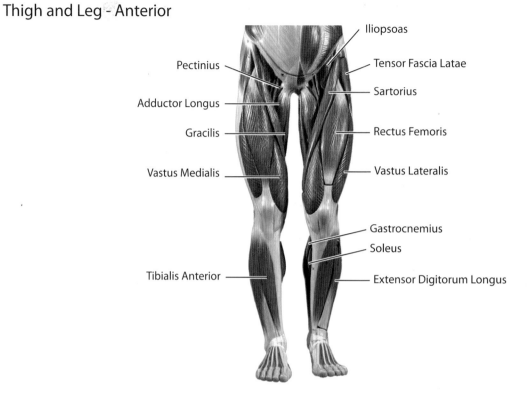

Pectinius

Adductor Longus

Gracilis

Vastus Medialis

Tibialis Anterior

Iliopsoas

Tensor Fascia Latae

Sartorius

Rectus Femoris

Vastus Lateralis

Gastrocnemius

Soleus

Extensor Digitorum Longus

Thigh and Leg - Posterior

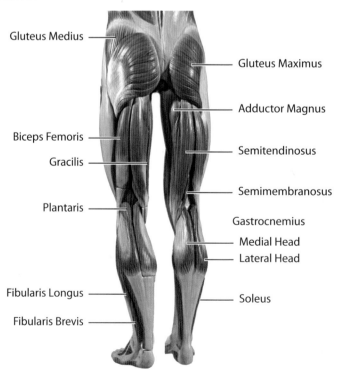

Gluteus Medius

Biceps Femoris

Gracilis

Plantaris

Fibularis Longus

Fibularis Brevis

Gluteus Maximus

Adductor Magnus

Semitendinosus

Semimembranosus

Gastrocnemius
Medial Head
Lateral Head

Soleus

Muscles of the Thigh and Leg

Thigh and Leg - Anterior

Thigh and Leg - Posterior

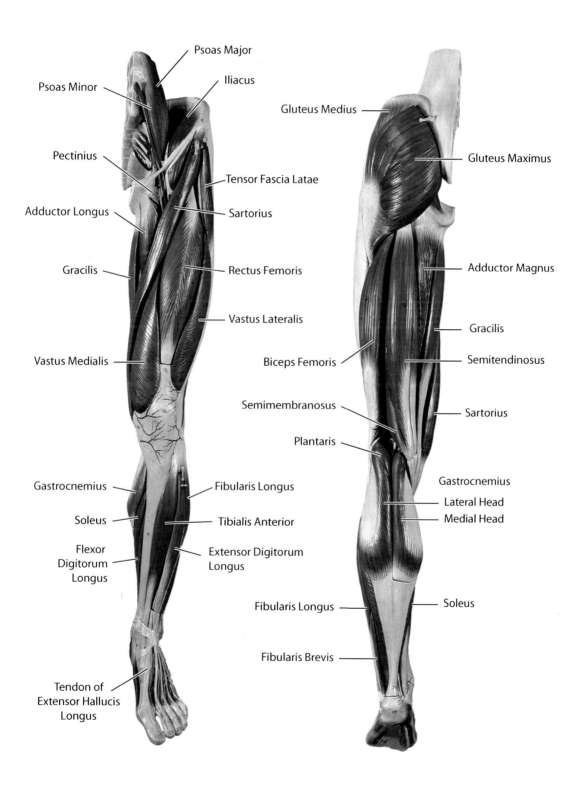

Psoas Major

Psoas Minor

Iliacus

Pectinius

Tensor Fascia Latae

Adductor Longus

Sartorius

Gracilis

Rectus Femoris

Vastus Lateralis

Vastus Medialis

Gastrocnemius

Fibularis Longus

Soleus

Tibialis Anterior

Flexor Digitorum Longus

Extensor Digitorum Longus

Tendon of Extensor Hallucis Longus

Gluteus Medius

Gluteus Maximus

Adductor Magnus

Gracilis

Semitendinosus

Biceps Femoris

Semimembranosus

Sartorius

Plantaris

Gastrocnemius

Lateral Head

Medial Head

Fibularis Longus

Soleus

Fibularis Brevis

Muscles of the Thigh and Leg

Thigh and Leg - Lateral

Thigh and Leg - Medial

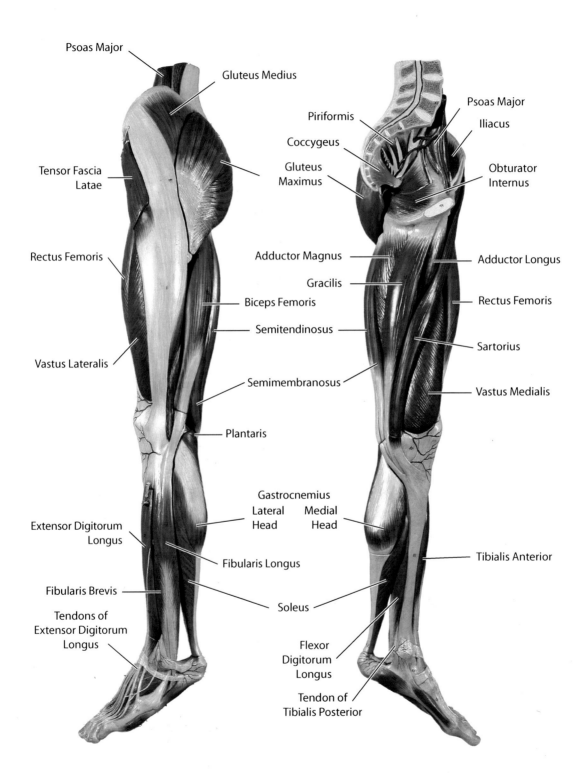

Psoas Major

Gluteus Medius

Piriformis

Coccygeus

Gluteus Maximus

Psoas Major

Iliacus

Tensor Fascia Latae

Obturator Internus

Rectus Femoris

Adductor Magnus

Gracilis

Biceps Femoris

Semitendinosus

Adductor Longus

Rectus Femoris

Sartorius

Vastus Lateralis

Semimembranosus

Vastus Medialis

Plantaris

Gastrocnemius
Lateral   Medial
Head   Head

Extensor Digitorum
Longus

Fibularis Longus

Tibialis Anterior

Fibularis Brevis

Soleus

Tendons of
Extensor Digitorum
Longus

Flexor
Digitorum
Longus

Tendon of
Tibialis Posterior

Muscles of the Thigh and Leg

Thigh and Leg - Posterior / Deep

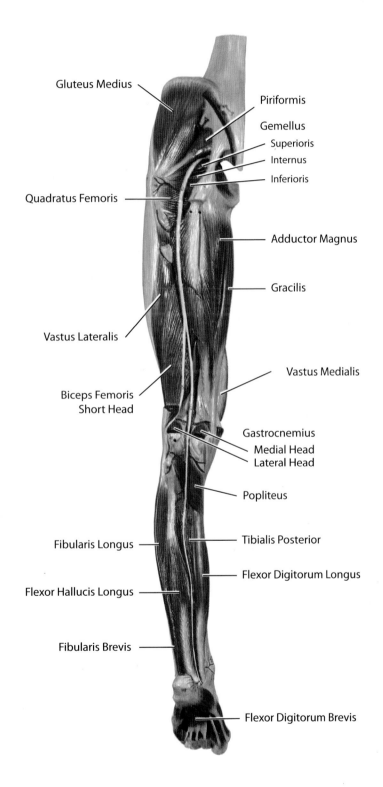

Gluteus Medius

Piriformis

Gemellus

Superioris

Internus

Inferioris

Quadratus Femoris

Adductor Magnus

Gracilis

Vastus Lateralis

Vastus Medialis

Biceps Femoris
Short Head

Gastrocnemius
Medial Head
Lateral Head

Popliteus

Fibularis Longus

Tibialis Posterior

Flexor Digitorum Longus

Flexor Hallucis Longus

Fibularis Brevis

Flexor Digitorum Brevis

Section 4

Nervous Tissue, Spinal Cord, Brain, and Sensory Organs

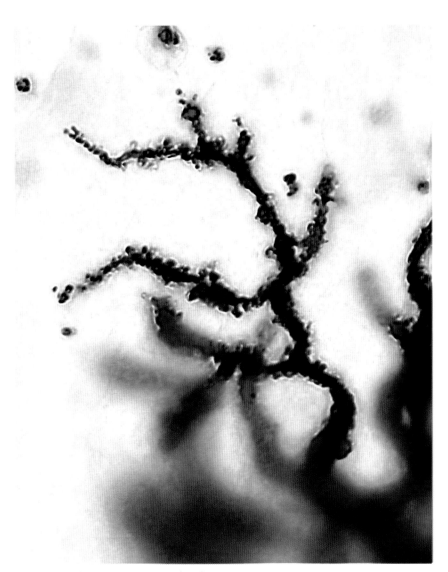

Dendrites of neuron showing dendritic spines (brightfield, silver; x1880)

Sensory and Motor Neurons

Unipolar Neuron (Sensory)

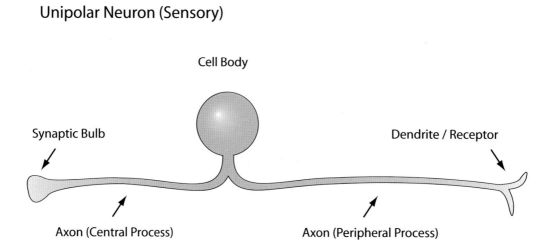

Cell Body

Synaptic Bulb

Dendrite / Receptor

Axon (Central Process)

Axon (Peripheral Process)

Multipolar Neuron (Motor)

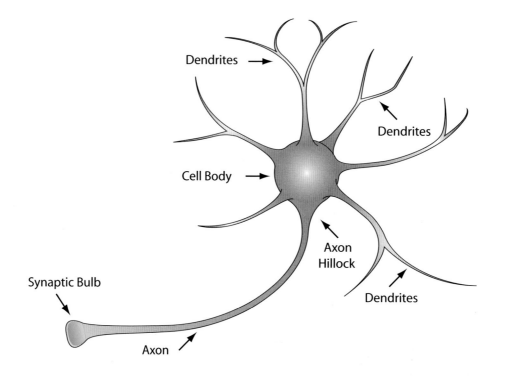

Dendrites

Dendrites

Cell Body

Axon
Hillock

Dendrites

Synaptic Bulb

Axon

Communication between Neurons

Synaptic Communication

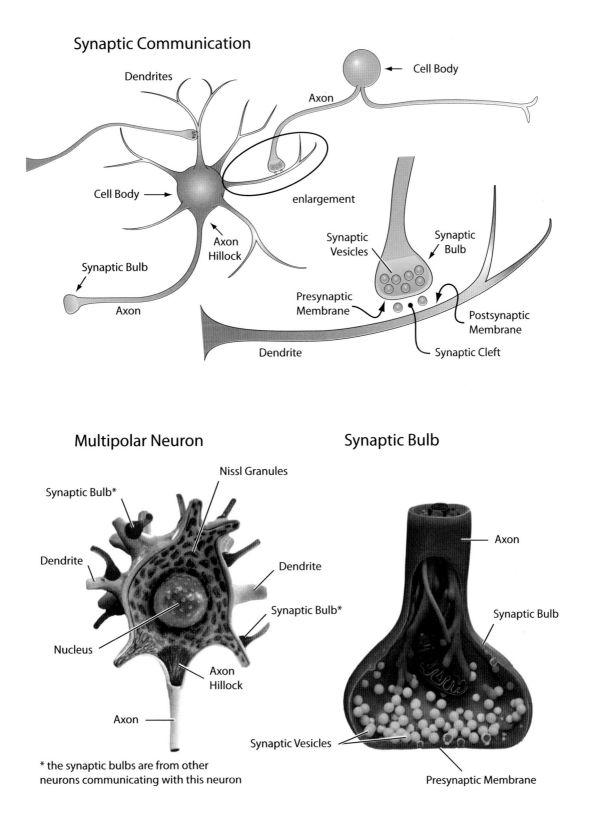

Cell Body

Dendrites

Axon

Cell Body

enlargement

Axon
Hillock

Synaptic Bulb

Axon

Synaptic
Vesicles

Synaptic
Bulb

Presynaptic
Membrane

Postsynaptic
Membrane

Synaptic Cleft

Dendrite

Multipolar Neuron

Synaptic Bulb*

Nissl Granules

Dendrite

Dendrite

Synaptic Bulb*

Nucleus

Axon
Hillock

Axon

* the synaptic bulbs are from other
neurons communicating with this neuron

Synaptic Bulb

Axon

Synaptic Bulb

Synaptic Vesicles

Presynaptic Membrane

Motor Neurons, Glial and Schwann Cells - with Histology

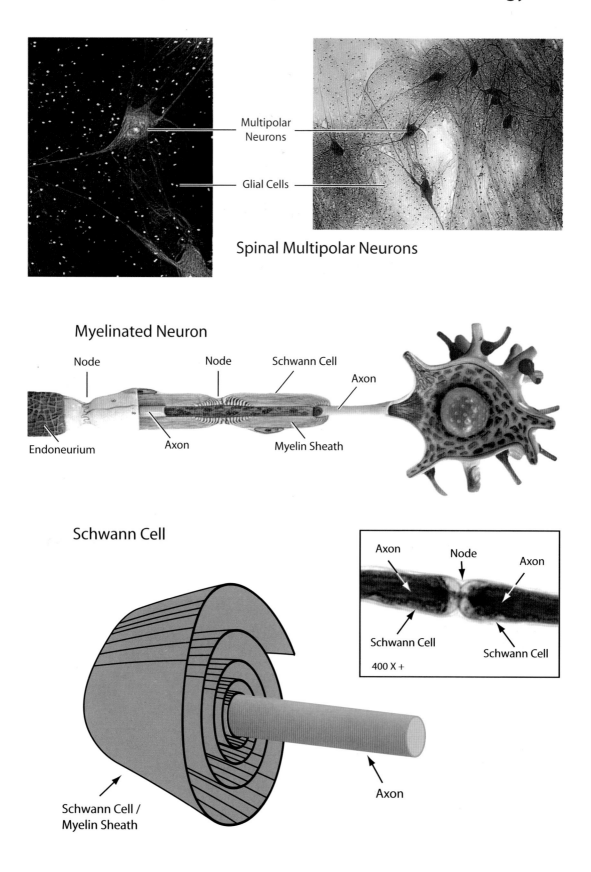

Multipolar Neurons

Glial Cells

Spinal Multipolar Neurons

Myelinated Neuron

Node

Node

Schwann Cell

Axon

Endoneurium

Axon

Myelin Sheath

Schwann Cell

Axon

Node

Axon

Schwann Cell

Schwann Cell

400 X +

Schwann Cell /
Myelin Sheath

Axon

Nerve and Schwann Cells - Histology

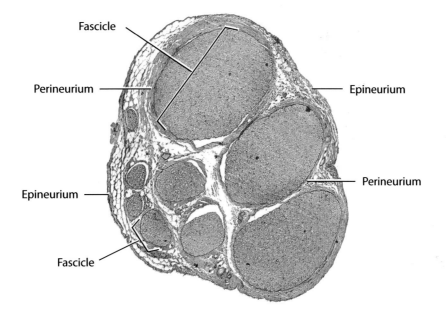

Fascicle

Perineurium

Epineurium

Epineurium

Perineurium

Fascicle

Nerve

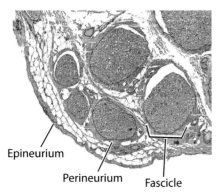

Epineurium

Perineurium

Fascicle

Nerve Fascicle

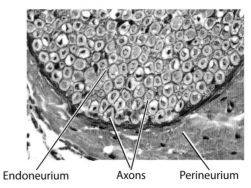

Endoneurium

Axons

Perineurium

Schwann Cells and Axons

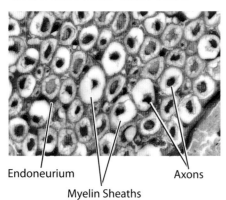

Endoneurium

Myelin Sheaths

Axons

Schwann Cells

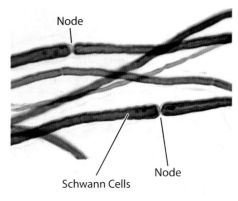

Node

Node

Schwann Cells

Neuromuscular Junctions and Motor Units - with Histology

Neuromuscular Junctions

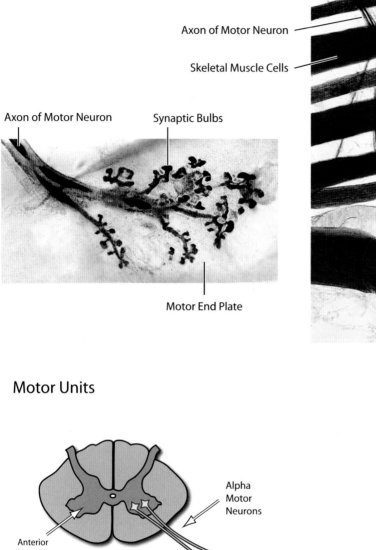

Axon of Motor Neuron

Skeletal Muscle Cells

Axon of Motor Neuron

Synaptic Bulbs

Motor End Plate

Motor End Plate

Motor Units

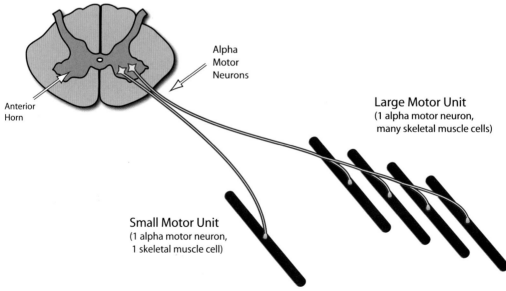

Alpha
Motor
Neurons

Anterior
Horn

Large Motor Unit
(1 alpha motor neuron,
many skeletal muscle cells)

Small Motor Unit
(1 alpha motor neuron,
1 skeletal muscle cell)

Spinal Cord

Anterior View

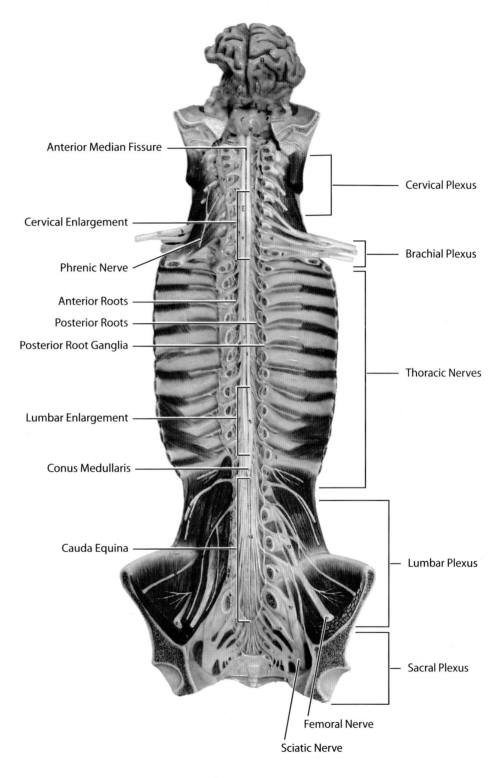

Anterior Median Fissure

Cervical Plexus

Cervical Enlargement

Phrenic Nerve

Brachial Plexus

Anterior Roots

Posterior Roots

Posterior Root Ganglia

Thoracic Nerves

Lumbar Enlargement

Conus Medullaris

Cauda Equina

Lumbar Plexus

Sacral Plexus

Femoral Nerve

Sciatic Nerve

Human Spinal Cord

Posterior View

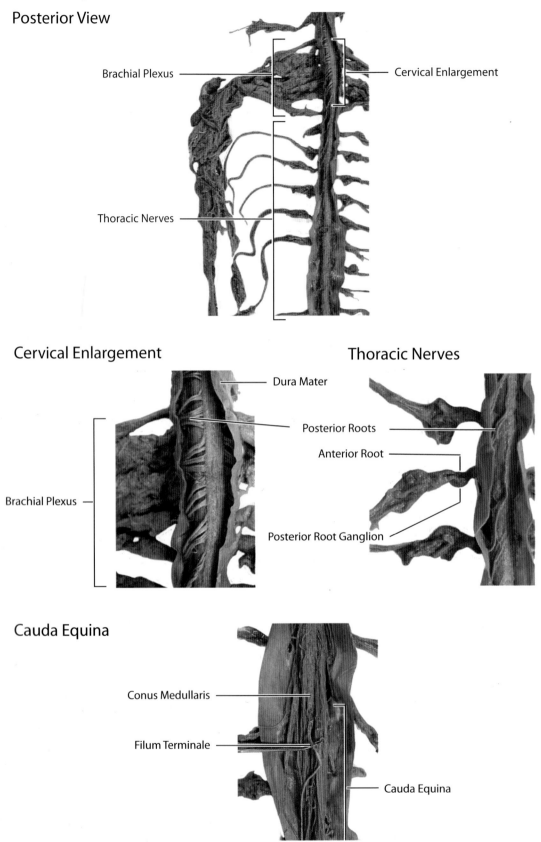

Brachial Plexus

Cervical Enlargement

Thoracic Nerves

Cervical Enlargement

Dura Mater

Posterior Roots

Brachial Plexus

Thoracic Nerves

Posterior Roots

Anterior Root

Posterior Root Ganglion

Cauda Equina

Conus Medullaris

Filum Terminale

Cauda Equina

Spinal Cord - with Histology

Cross Section with Meninges

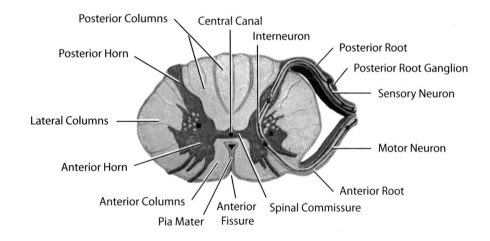

Spinal Commissure
Central Canal
Posterior Columns
Posterior Horn
Lateral Columns
Posterior Root
Denticulate Ligament
Anterior Horn
Anterior Columns
Anterior Root
Dura Mater
Pia Mater
Arachnoid

Cross Section without Meninges

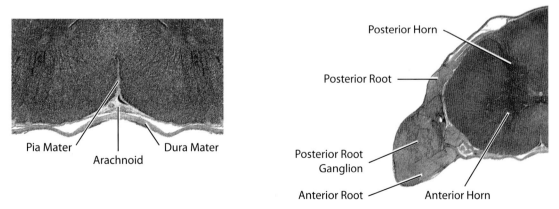

Posterior Columns
Central Canal
Interneuron
Posterior Horn
Posterior Root
Posterior Root Ganglion
Sensory Neuron
Lateral Columns
Motor Neuron
Anterior Horn
Anterior Columns
Anterior Root
Pia Mater
Anterior Fissure
Spinal Commissure

Meninges

Pia Mater
Arachnoid
Dura Mater

Horns and Roots

Posterior Horn
Posterior Root
Posterior Root Ganglion
Anterior Root
Anterior Horn

Spinal Cord - Histology

Meninges

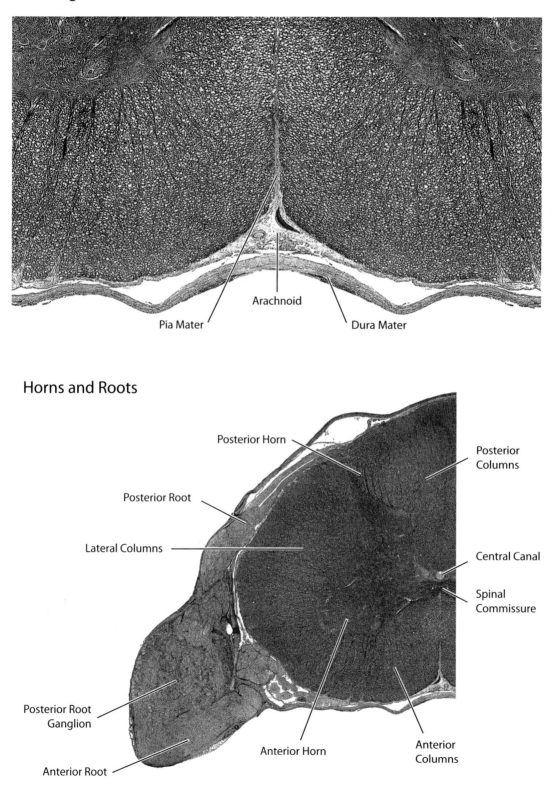

Arachnoid

Pia Mater

Dura Mater

Horns and Roots

Posterior Horn

Posterior Columns

Posterior Root

Lateral Columns

Central Canal

Spinal Commissure

Posterior Root Ganglion

Anterior Root

Anterior Horn

Anterior Columns

Dermatomes and Stretch Reflex

Dermatomes

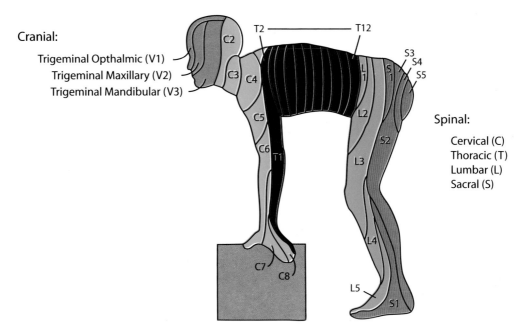

Cranial:

Trigeminal Opthalmic (V1)
Trigeminal Maxillary (V2)
Trigeminal Mandibular (V3)

Spinal:

Cervical (C)
Thoracic (T)
Lumbar (L)
Sacral (S)

Spinal Stretch Reflex

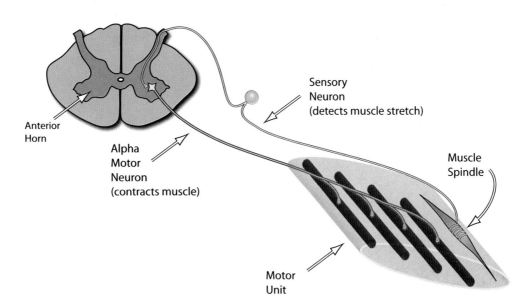

Anterior Horn

Alpha Motor Neuron (contracts muscle)

Sensory Neuron (detects muscle stretch)

Muscle Spindle

Motor Unit

Dura Mater and Cerebral Cortex

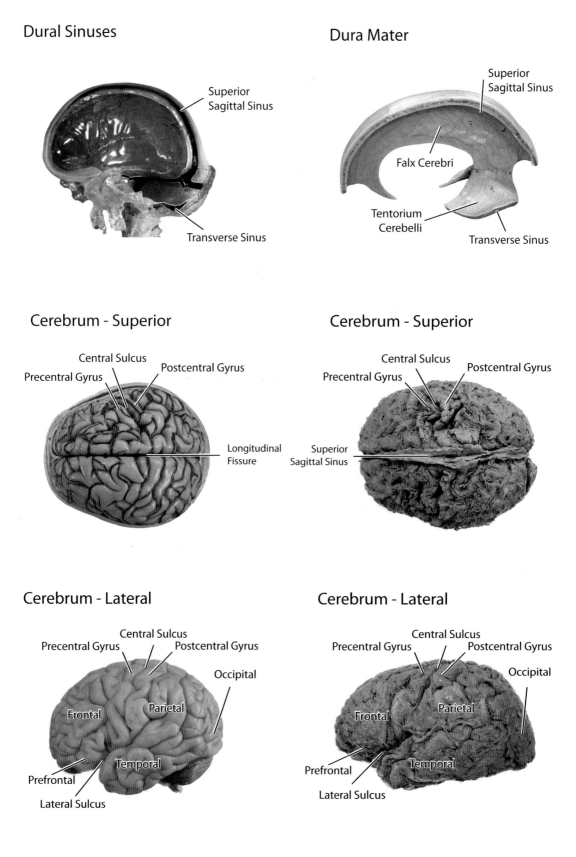

Dural Sinuses

Superior Sagittal Sinus

Transverse Sinus

Dura Mater

Superior Sagittal Sinus

Falx Cerebri

Tentorium Cerebelli

Transverse Sinus

Cerebrum - Superior

Central Sulcus

Precentral Gyrus

Postcentral Gyrus

Longitudinal Fissure

Cerebrum - Superior

Central Sulcus

Precentral Gyrus

Postcentral Gyrus

Superior Sagittal Sinus

Cerebrum - Lateral

Precentral Gyrus

Central Sulcus

Postcentral Gyrus

Occipital

Frontal

Parietal

Prefrontal

Temporal

Lateral Sulcus

Cerebrum - Lateral

Precentral Gyrus

Central Sulcus

Postcentral Gyrus

Occipital

Frontal

Parietal

Prefrontal

Temporal

Lateral Sulcus

Cerebral Cortex

Functional Regions

Primary Motor Cortex

Premotor Area

Primary Somatosensory Cortex

Posterior Parietal Cortex

Visual Cortex

Prefrontal Cortex

Supplementary Motor Area

Primary Auditory Cortex

Somatotopic Map of Motor Cortex

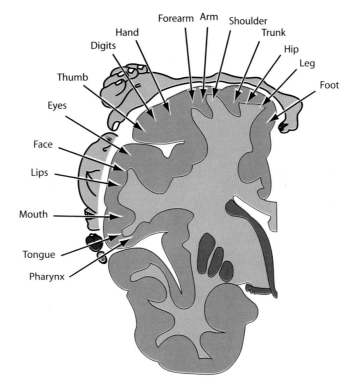

Forearm Arm Shoulder Trunk

Hand

Digits

Hip

Leg

Thumb

Foot

Eyes

Face

Lips

Mouth

Tongue

Pharynx

Brain and Cranial Nerves

Brain - Inferior

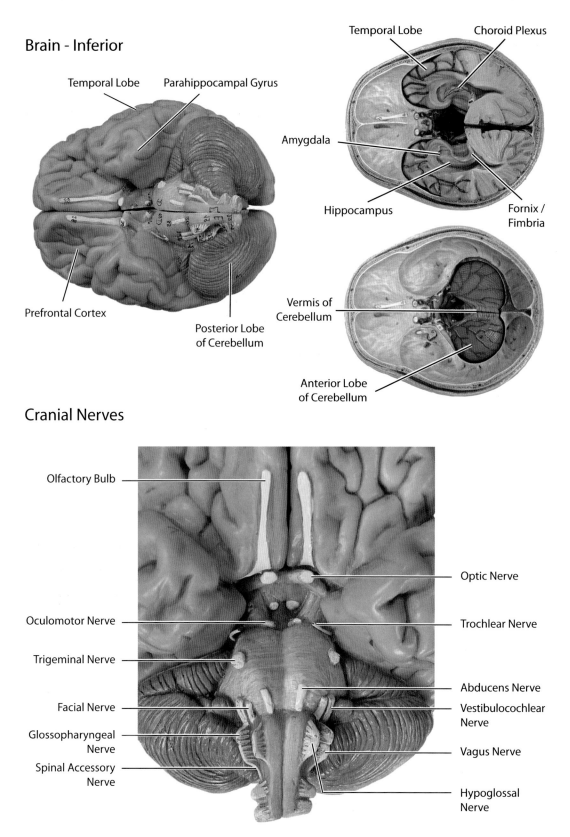

Temporal Lobe

Parahippocampal Gyrus

Prefrontal Cortex

Posterior Lobe of Cerebellum

Temporal Lobe

Choroid Plexus

Amygdala

Hippocampus

Fornix / Fimbria

Vermis of Cerebellum

Anterior Lobe of Cerebellum

Cranial Nerves

Olfactory Bulb

Oculomotor Nerve

Trigeminal Nerve

Facial Nerve

Glossopharyngeal Nerve

Spinal Accessory Nerve

Optic Nerve

Trochlear Nerve

Abducens Nerve

Vestibulocochlear Nerve

Vagus Nerve

Hypoglossal Nerve

Section 4 • Nervous Tissue, Spinal Cord, Brain, and Sensory Organs

Brain and Brainstem

Brain - Midsagittal

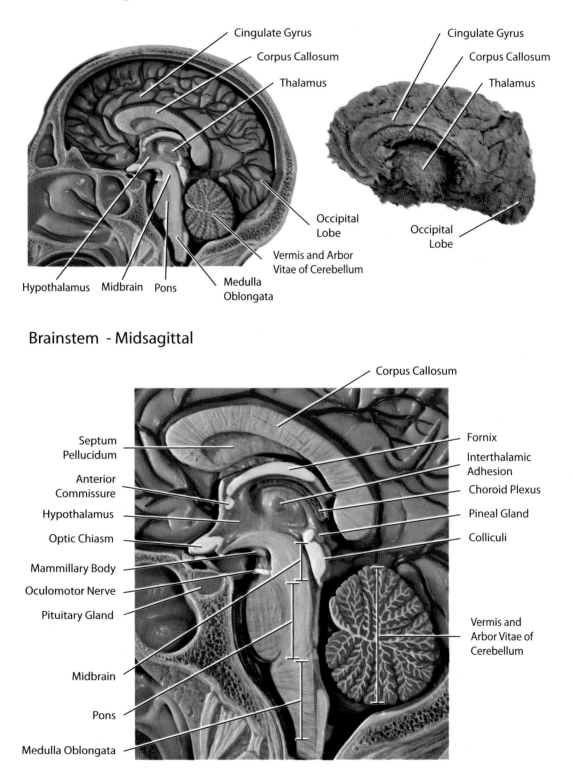

Cingulate Gyrus

Corpus Callosum

Thalamus

Cingulate Gyrus

Corpus Callosum

Thalamus

Occipital Lobe

Occipital Lobe

Vermis and Arbor Vitae of Cerebellum

Hypothalamus Midbrain Pons Medulla Oblongata

Brainstem - Midsagittal

Corpus Callosum

Septum Pellucidum

Anterior Commissure

Hypothalamus

Optic Chiasm

Mammillary Body

Oculomotor Nerve

Pituitary Gland

Midbrain

Pons

Medulla Oblongata

Fornix

Interthalamic Adhesion

Choroid Plexus

Pineal Gland

Colliculi

Vermis and Arbor Vitae of Cerebellum

Ventricles of the Brain and Basal Nuclei

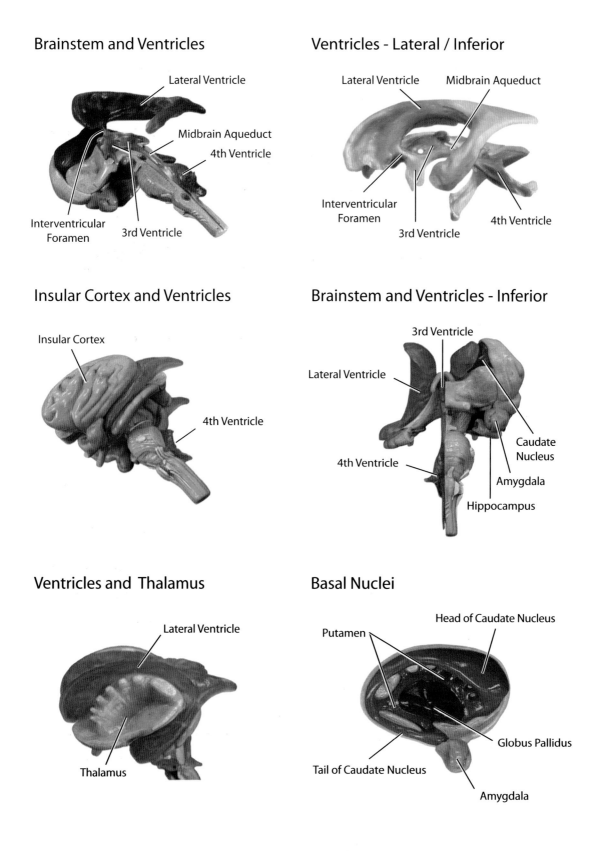

Brainstem and Ventricles

Lateral Ventricle

Midbrain Aqueduct

4th Ventricle

Interventricular Foramen

3rd Ventricle

Ventricles - Lateral / Inferior

Lateral Ventricle

Midbrain Aqueduct

Interventricular Foramen

3rd Ventricle

4th Ventricle

Insular Cortex and Ventricles

Insular Cortex

4th Ventricle

Brainstem and Ventricles - Inferior

3rd Ventricle

Lateral Ventricle

Caudate Nucleus

4th Ventricle

Amygdala

Hippocampus

Ventricles and Thalamus

Lateral Ventricle

Thalamus

Basal Nuclei

Head of Caudate Nucleus

Putamen

Globus Pallidus

Tail of Caudate Nucleus

Amygdala

Brainstem and Limbic Structures

Brainstem - Superior

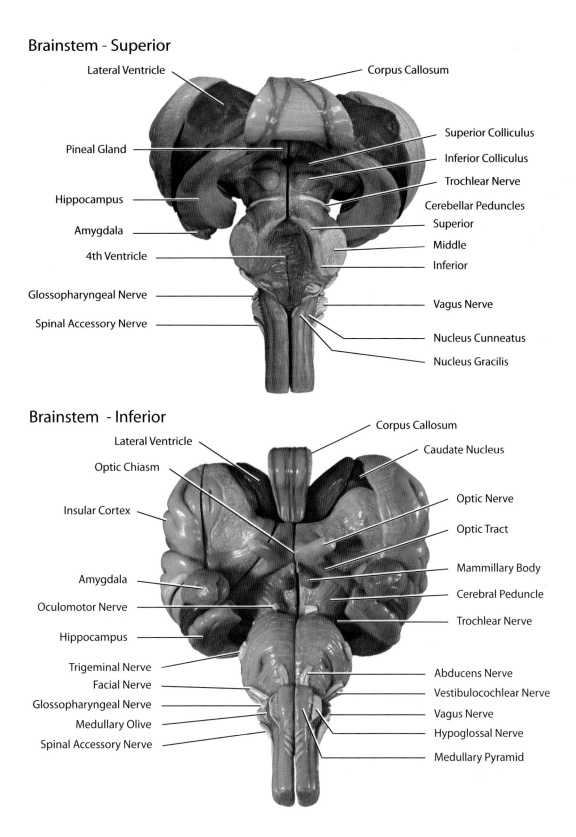

Lateral Ventricle
Corpus Callosum
Pineal Gland
Superior Colliculus
Inferior Colliculus
Trochlear Nerve
Cerebellar Peduncles
Hippocampus
Superior
Amygdala
Middle
4th Ventricle
Inferior
Glossopharyngeal Nerve
Vagus Nerve
Spinal Accessory Nerve
Nucleus Cunneatus
Nucleus Gracilis

Brainstem - Inferior

Corpus Callosum
Lateral Ventricle
Optic Chiasm
Caudate Nucleus
Insular Cortex
Optic Nerve
Optic Tract
Amygdala
Mammillary Body
Oculomotor Nerve
Cerebral Peduncle
Hippocampus
Trochlear Nerve
Trigeminal Nerve
Facial Nerve
Abducens Nerve
Glossopharyngeal Nerve
Vestibulocochlear Nerve
Medullary Olive
Vagus Nerve
Spinal Accessory Nerve
Hypoglossal Nerve
Medullary Pyramid

Dura Mater and Brain of Sheep

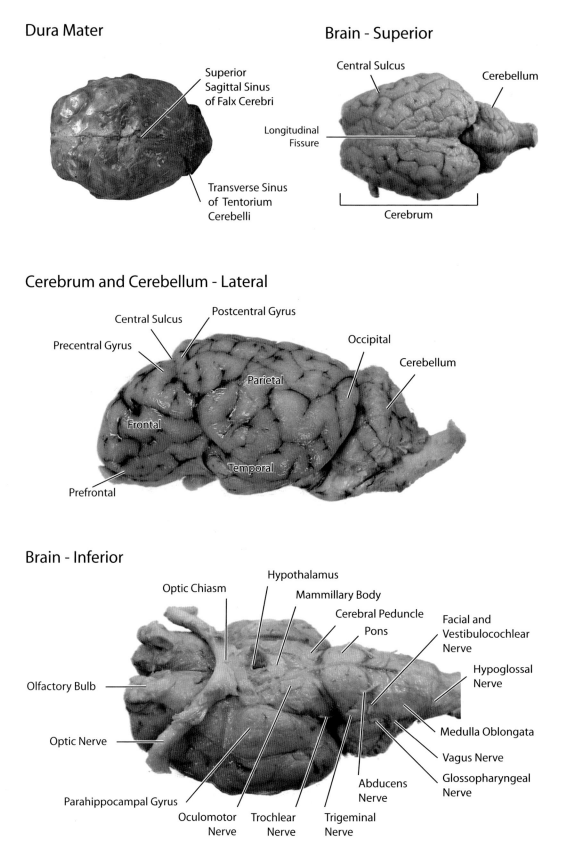

Dura Mater

Superior
Sagittal Sinus
of Falx Cerebri

Transverse Sinus
of Tentorium
Cerebelli

Brain - Superior

Central Sulcus

Cerebellum

Longitudinal
Fissure

Cerebrum

Cerebrum and Cerebellum - Lateral

Central Sulcus

Postcentral Gyrus

Precentral Gyrus

Occipital

Cerebellum

Parietal

Frontal

Temporal

Prefrontal

Brain - Inferior

Optic Chiasm

Hypothalamus

Mammillary Body

Cerebral Peduncle

Pons

Facial and
Vestibulocochlear
Nerve

Hypoglossal
Nerve

Olfactory Bulb

Optic Nerve

Medulla Oblongata

Vagus Nerve

Glossopharyngeal
Nerve

Parahippocampal Gyrus

Oculomotor
Nerve

Trochlear
Nerve

Trigeminal
Nerve

Abducens
Nerve

Brain of Sheep

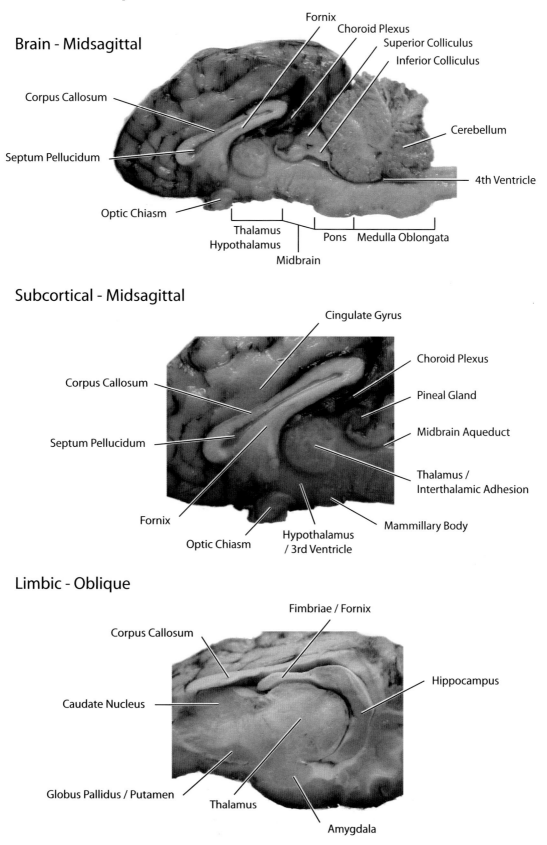

Brain - Midsagittal

Fornix
Choroid Plexus
Superior Colliculus
Inferior Colliculus

Corpus Callosum

Cerebellum

Septum Pellucidum

4th Ventricle

Optic Chiasm

Thalamus
Hypothalamus

Pons   Medulla Oblongata

Midbrain

Subcortical - Midsagittal

Cingulate Gyrus

Choroid Plexus

Corpus Callosum

Pineal Gland

Midbrain Aqueduct

Septum Pellucidum

Thalamus /
Interthalamic Adhesion

Fornix

Mammillary Body

Optic Chiasm

Hypothalamus
/ 3rd Ventricle

Limbic - Oblique

Fimbriae / Fornix

Corpus Callosum

Hippocampus

Caudate Nucleus

Globus Pallidus / Putamen

Thalamus

Amygdala

Sensory Neurons and Receptors

Large and Small Sensory Neurons

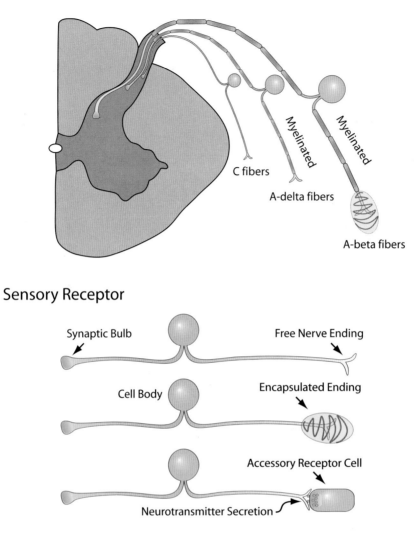

Myelinated

Myelinated

C fibers

A-delta fibers

A-beta fibers

Sensory Receptor

Synaptic Bulb

Free Nerve Ending

Cell Body

Encapsulated Ending

Accessory Receptor Cell

Neurotransmitter Secretion

Encapsulated Receptors

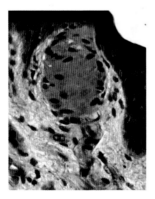

Meissner's Corpuscle

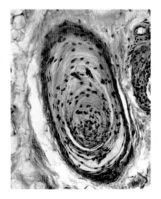

Pacinian Corpuscle

Ear and Cochlea

Ear

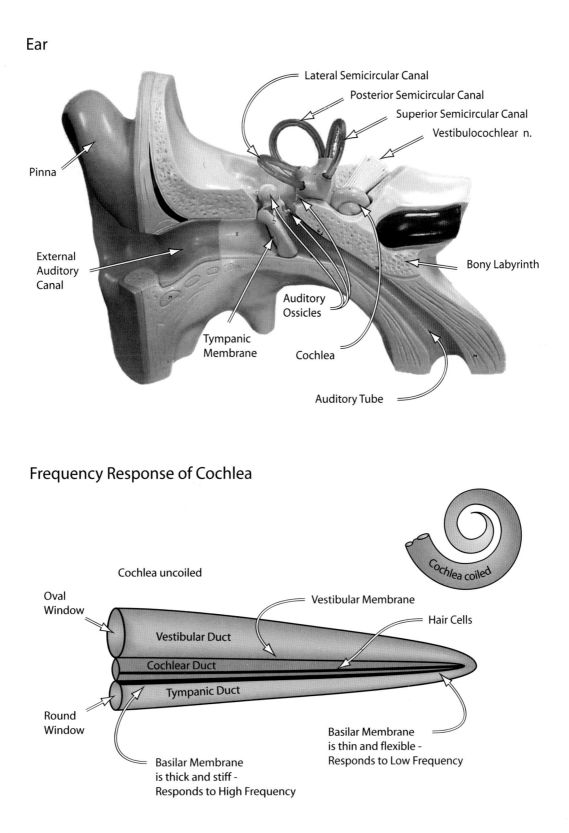

Lateral Semicircular Canal

Posterior Semicircular Canal

Superior Semicircular Canal

Vestibulocochlear n.

Pinna

External
Auditory
Canal

Bony Labyrinth

Auditory
Ossicles

Tympanic
Membrane

Cochlea

Auditory Tube

Frequency Response of Cochlea

Cochlea coiled

Cochlea uncoiled

Oval
Window

Vestibular Membrane

Hair Cells

Vestibular Duct

Cochlear Duct

Tympanic Duct

Round
Window

Basilar Membrane
is thin and flexible -
Responds to Low Frequency

Basilar Membrane
is thick and stiff -
Responds to High Frequency

Cochlea - Histology

Cochlea

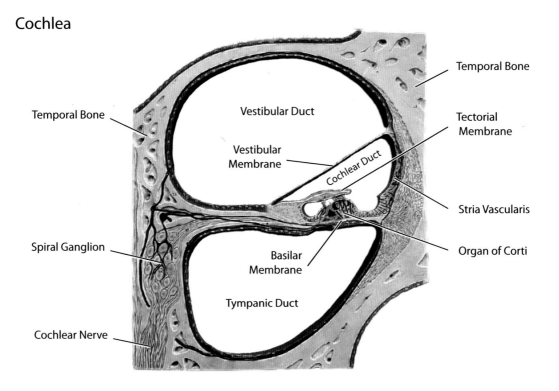

Temporal Bone

Temporal Bone

Vestibular Duct

Vestibular Membrane

Cochlear Duct

Tectorial Membrane

Stria Vascularis

Spiral Ganglion

Basilar Membrane

Organ of Corti

Tympanic Duct

Cochlear Nerve

Cochlea

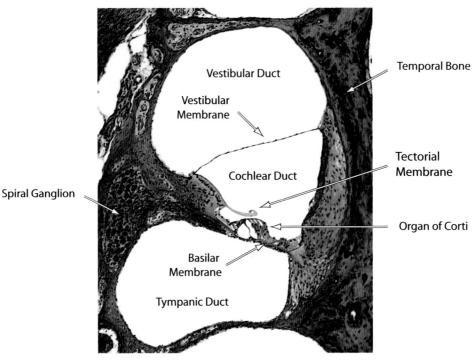

Vestibular Duct

Vestibular Membrane

Temporal Bone

Cochlear Duct

Tectorial Membrane

Spiral Ganglion

Organ of Corti

Basilar Membrane

Tympanic Duct

Cochlea and Vestibular Apparatus - with Histology

Organ of Corti

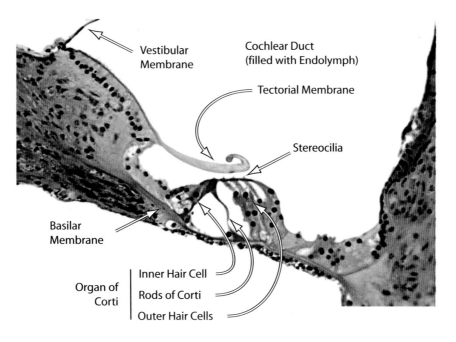

Vestibular Membrane

Cochlear Duct (filled with Endolymph)

Tectorial Membrane

Stereocilia

Basilar Membrane

Organ of Corti
- Inner Hair Cell
- Rods of Corti
- Outer Hair Cells

Vestibular Apparatus and Cochlea - Posterior View

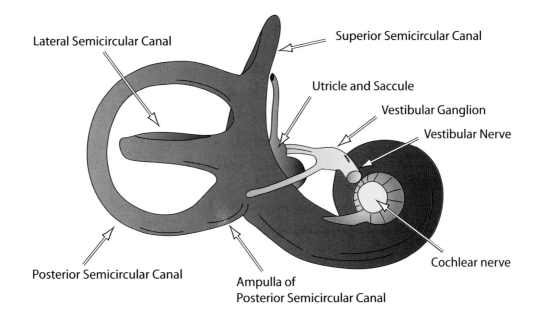

Lateral Semicircular Canal

Superior Semicircular Canal

Utricle and Saccule

Vestibular Ganglion

Vestibular Nerve

Cochlear nerve

Posterior Semicircular Canal

Ampulla of Posterior Semicircular Canal

Eye

Eye - Midsagittal

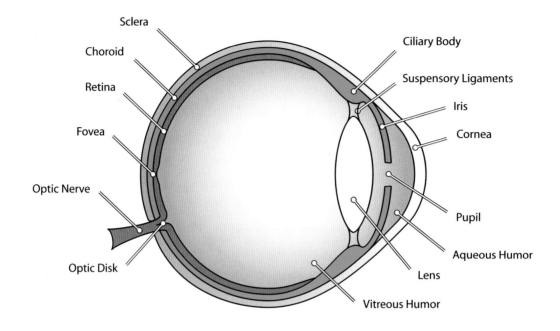

Sclera
Choroid
Retina
Fovea
Optic Nerve
Optic Disk

Ciliary Body
Suspensory Ligaments
Iris
Cornea
Pupil
Aqueous Humor
Lens
Vitreous Humor

Eye - Anterior

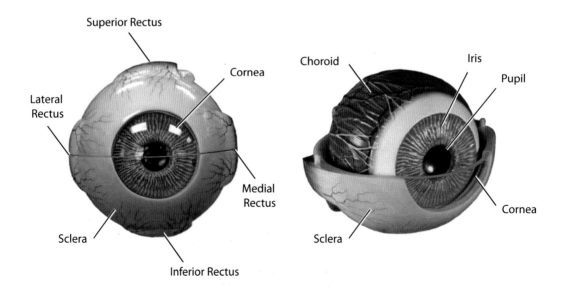

Superior Rectus
Cornea
Lateral Rectus
Medial Rectus
Sclera
Inferior Rectus

Choroid
Iris
Pupil
Cornea
Sclera

Eye and Retina - with Histology

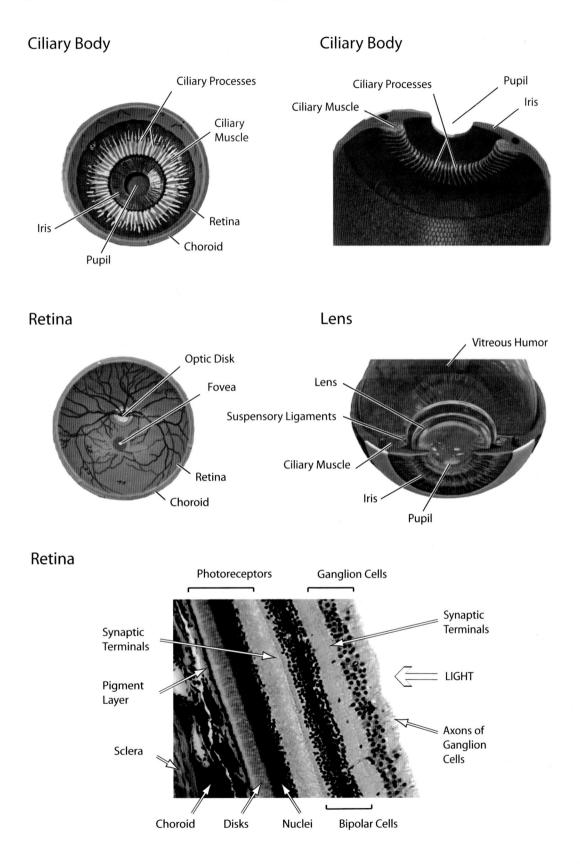

Ciliary Body

Ciliary Processes
Ciliary Muscle
Iris
Pupil
Retina
Choroid

Ciliary Body

Ciliary Muscle
Ciliary Processes
Pupil
Iris

Retina

Optic Disk
Fovea
Retina
Choroid

Lens

Vitreous Humor
Lens
Suspensory Ligaments
Ciliary Muscle
Iris
Pupil

Retina

Photoreceptors
Ganglion Cells
Synaptic Terminals
Synaptic Terminals
LIGHT
Pigment Layer
Axons of Ganglion Cells
Sclera
Choroid
Disks
Nuclei
Bipolar Cells

Section 5

Heart, Blood Vessels, and Blood

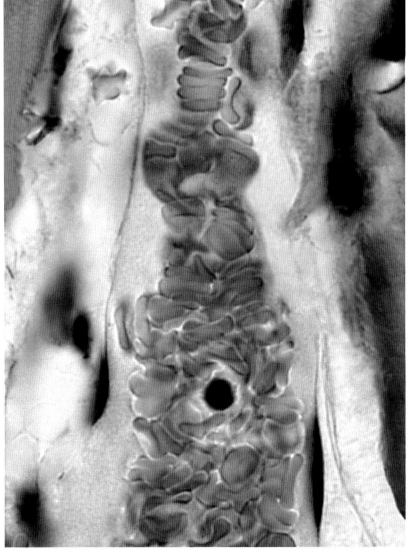

Erythrocytes in blood vessel in spongy bone (brightfield, H&E; x1880)

Overview of the Circulation

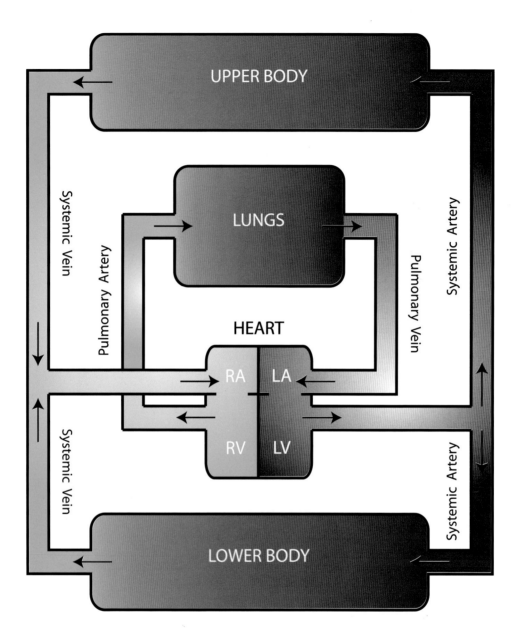

Thoracic Cavity and Organization of the Heart

Thoracic Cavity

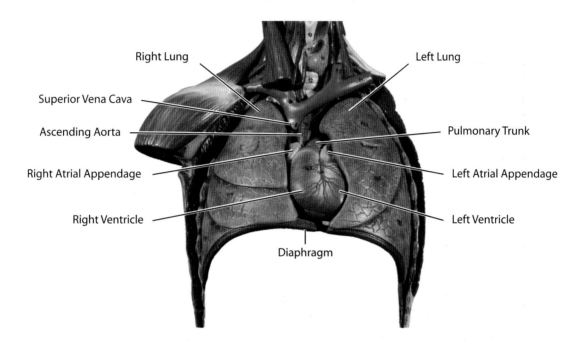

Right Lung

Left Lung

Superior Vena Cava

Ascending Aorta

Pulmonary Trunk

Right Atrial Appendage

Left Atrial Appendage

Right Ventricle

Left Ventricle

Diaphragm

Organization of the Heart

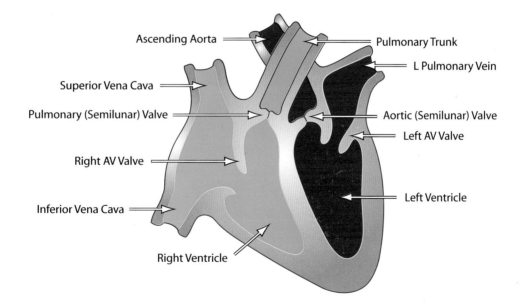

Ascending Aorta

Pulmonary Trunk

L Pulmonary Vein

Superior Vena Cava

Pulmonary (Semilunar) Valve

Aortic (Semilunar) Valve

Left AV Valve

Right AV Valve

Inferior Vena Cava

Left Ventricle

Right Ventricle

Heart

Heart - Anterior

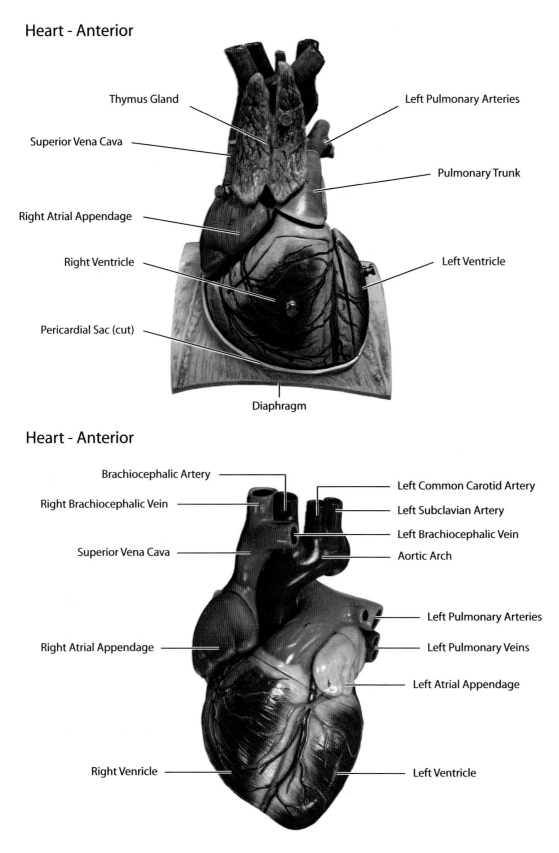

Thymus Gland

Superior Vena Cava

Right Atrial Appendage

Right Ventricle

Pericardial Sac (cut)

Left Pulmonary Arteries

Pulmonary Trunk

Left Ventricle

Diaphragm

Heart - Anterior

Brachiocephalic Artery

Right Brachiocephalic Vein

Superior Vena Cava

Right Atrial Appendage

Right Venricle

Left Common Carotid Artery

Left Subclavian Artery

Left Brachiocephalic Vein

Aortic Arch

Left Pulmonary Arteries

Left Pulmonary Veins

Left Atrial Appendage

Left Ventricle

Heart

Heart - Posterior / Inferior

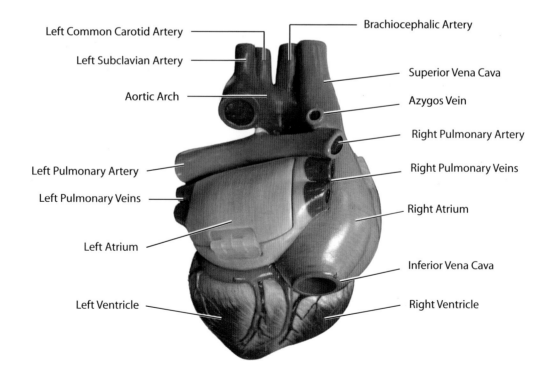

Right Pulmonary Artery

Right Pulmonary Vein

Inferior Vena Cava

Right Atrium

Left Atrium

Left Pulmonary Artery

Left Pulmonary Vein

Left Ventricle

Right Ventricle

Apex

Heart - Posterior

Left Common Carotid Artery

Left Subclavian Artery

Aortic Arch

Brachiocephalic Artery

Superior Vena Cava

Azygos Vein

Right Pulmonary Artery

Left Pulmonary Artery

Right Pulmonary Veins

Left Pulmonary Veins

Right Atrium

Left Atrium

Inferior Vena Cava

Left Ventricle

Right Ventricle

Heart

Heart - Right

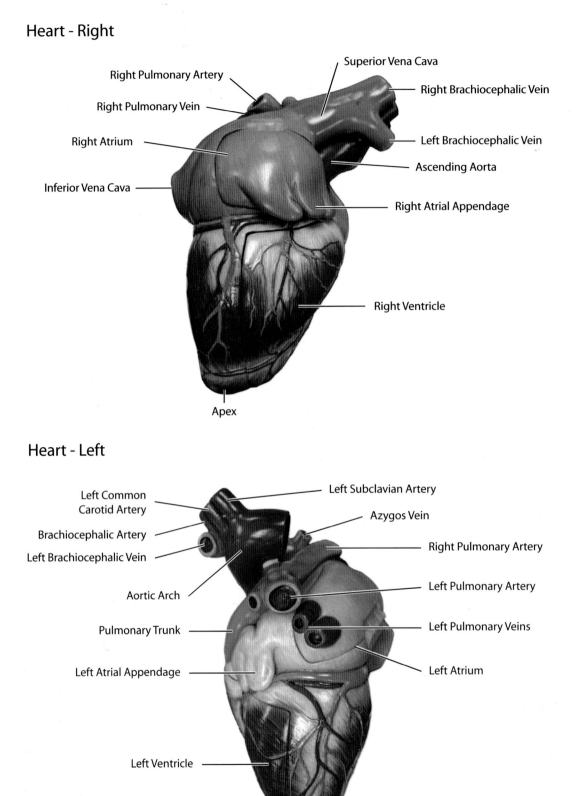

Right Pulmonary Artery

Right Pulmonary Vein

Right Atrium

Inferior Vena Cava

Superior Vena Cava

Right Brachiocephalic Vein

Left Brachiocephalic Vein

Ascending Aorta

Right Atrial Appendage

Right Ventricle

Apex

Heart - Left

Left Common Carotid Artery

Brachiocephalic Artery

Left Brachiocephalic Vein

Aortic Arch

Pulmonary Trunk

Left Atrial Appendage

Left Ventricle

Left Subclavian Artery

Azygos Vein

Right Pulmonary Artery

Left Pulmonary Artery

Left Pulmonary Veins

Left Atrium

Pig Heart

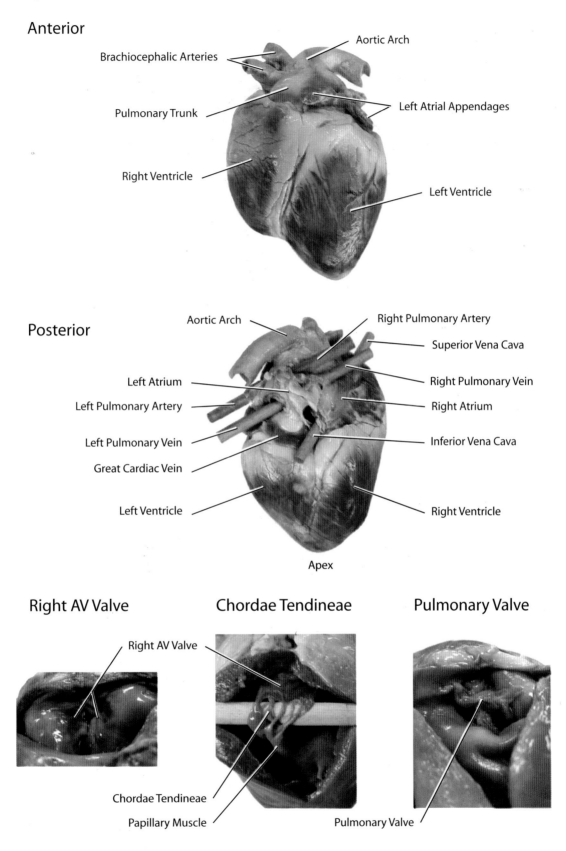

Anterior

Brachiocephalic Arteries

Aortic Arch

Pulmonary Trunk

Left Atrial Appendages

Right Ventricle

Left Ventricle

Posterior

Aortic Arch

Right Pulmonary Artery

Superior Vena Cava

Left Atrium

Right Pulmonary Vein

Left Pulmonary Artery

Right Atrium

Left Pulmonary Vein

Inferior Vena Cava

Great Cardiac Vein

Left Ventricle

Right Ventricle

Apex

Right AV Valve

Right AV Valve

Chordae Tendineae

Chordae Tendineae

Papillary Muscle

Pulmonary Valve

Pulmonary Valve

Heart - Interior

Right

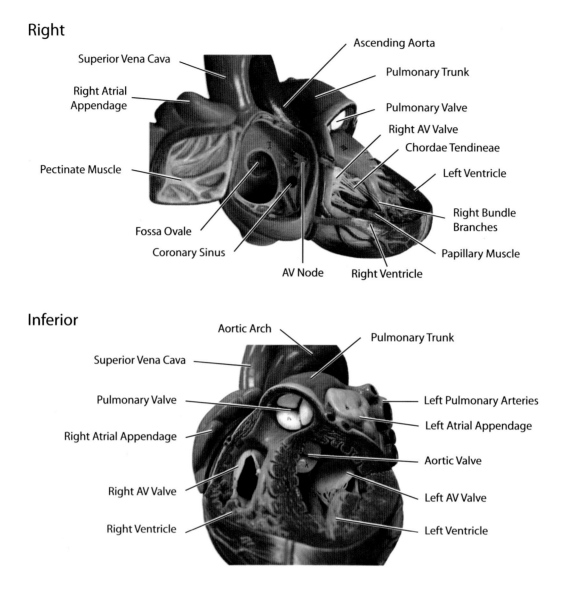

Superior Vena Cava
Right Atrial Appendage
Pectinate Muscle
Fossa Ovale
Coronary Sinus
AV Node
Ascending Aorta
Pulmonary Trunk
Pulmonary Valve
Right AV Valve
Chordae Tendineae
Left Ventricle
Right Bundle Branches
Papillary Muscle
Right Ventricle

Inferior

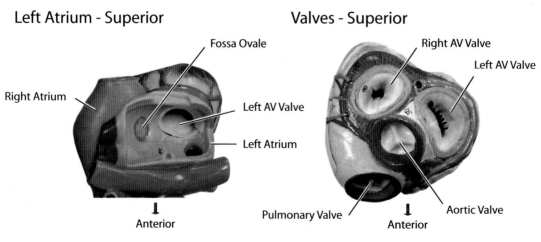

Aortic Arch
Superior Vena Cava
Pulmonary Valve
Right Atrial Appendage
Right AV Valve
Right Ventricle
Pulmonary Trunk
Left Pulmonary Arteries
Left Atrial Appendage
Aortic Valve
Left AV Valve
Left Ventricle

Left Atrium - Superior

Right Atrium
Fossa Ovale
Left AV Valve
Left Atrium

↓
Anterior

Valves - Superior

Right AV Valve
Left AV Valve
Pulmonary Valve
Aortic Valve

↓
Anterior

Coronary Arteries and Veins

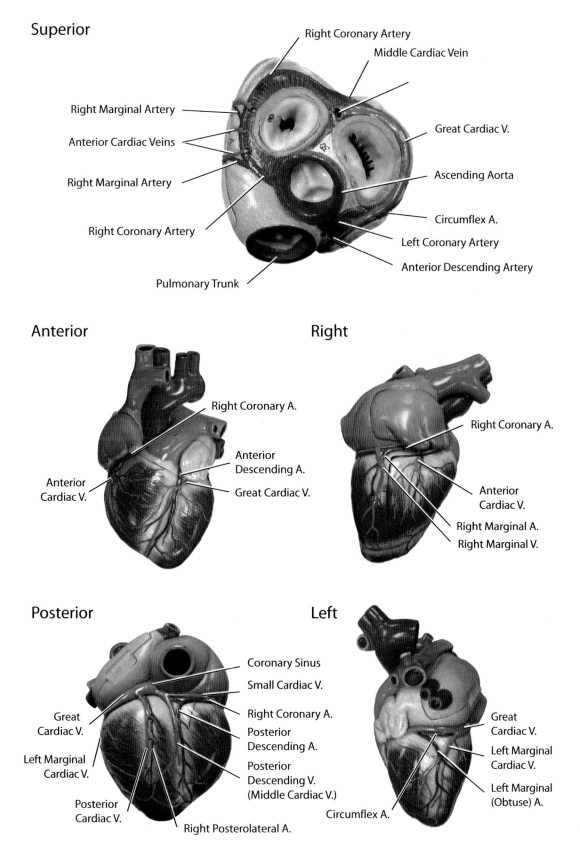

Superior

Right Coronary Artery

Middle Cardiac Vein

Right Marginal Artery

Anterior Cardiac Veins

Right Marginal Artery

Great Cardiac V.

Ascending Aorta

Right Coronary Artery

Circumflex A.

Left Coronary Artery

Anterior Descending Artery

Pulmonary Trunk

Anterior

Right Coronary A.

Anterior Descending A.

Great Cardiac V.

Anterior Cardiac V.

Right

Right Coronary A.

Anterior Cardiac V.

Right Marginal A.

Right Marginal V.

Posterior

Coronary Sinus

Small Cardiac V.

Right Coronary A.

Posterior Descending A.

Posterior Descending V. (Middle Cardiac V.)

Great Cardiac V.

Left Marginal Cardiac V.

Posterior Cardiac V.

Right Posterolateral A.

Left

Great Cardiac V.

Left Marginal Cardiac V.

Left Marginal (Obtuse) A.

Circumflex A.

Heart Wall, Valves and Cardiac Muscle - Histology

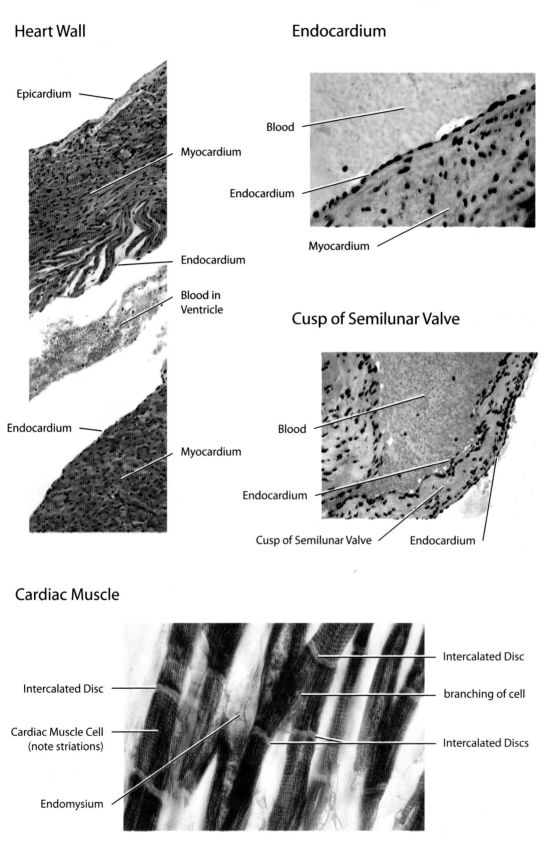

Heart Wall

Epicardium

Myocardium

Endocardium

Blood in Ventricle

Endocardium

Myocardium

Endocardium

Blood

Endocardium

Myocardium

Cusp of Semilunar Valve

Blood

Endocardium

Cusp of Semilunar Valve

Endocardium

Cardiac Muscle

Intercalated Disc

Cardiac Muscle Cell (note striations)

Endomysium

Intercalated Disc

branching of cell

Intercalated Discs

Arteries and Veins - Head and Neck

Trunk, Neck and Head

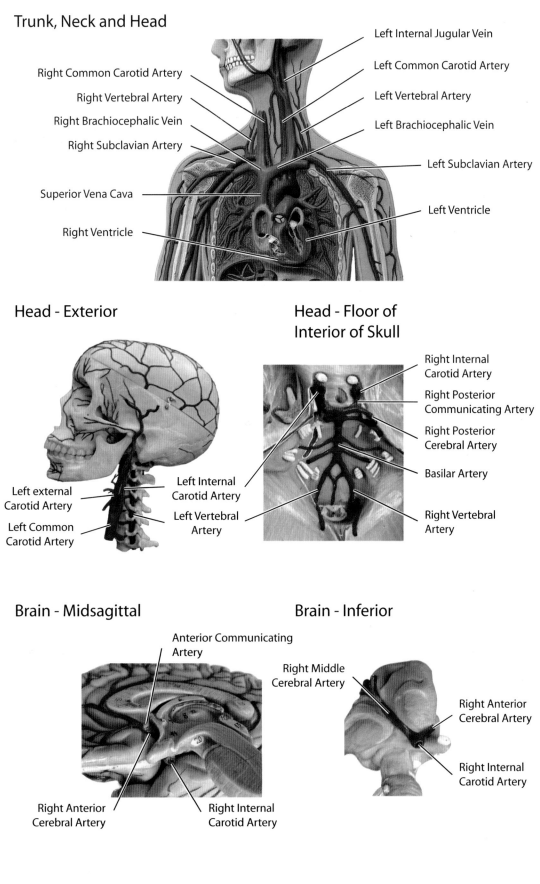

Left Internal Jugular Vein

Right Common Carotid Artery

Left Common Carotid Artery

Right Vertebral Artery

Left Vertebral Artery

Right Brachiocephalic Vein

Left Brachiocephalic Vein

Right Subclavian Artery

Left Subclavian Artery

Superior Vena Cava

Left Ventricle

Right Ventricle

Head - Exterior

Left external Carotid Artery

Left Internal Carotid Artery

Left Common Carotid Artery

Left Vertebral Artery

Head - Floor of Interior of Skull

Right Internal Carotid Artery

Right Posterior Communicating Artery

Right Posterior Cerebral Artery

Basilar Artery

Right Vertebral Artery

Brain - Midsagittal

Anterior Communicating Artery

Right Anterior Cerebral Artery

Right Internal Carotid Artery

Brain - Inferior

Right Middle Cerebral Artery

Right Anterior Cerebral Artery

Right Internal Carotid Artery

Arteries and Veins - Trunk and Arm

Trunk and Arm

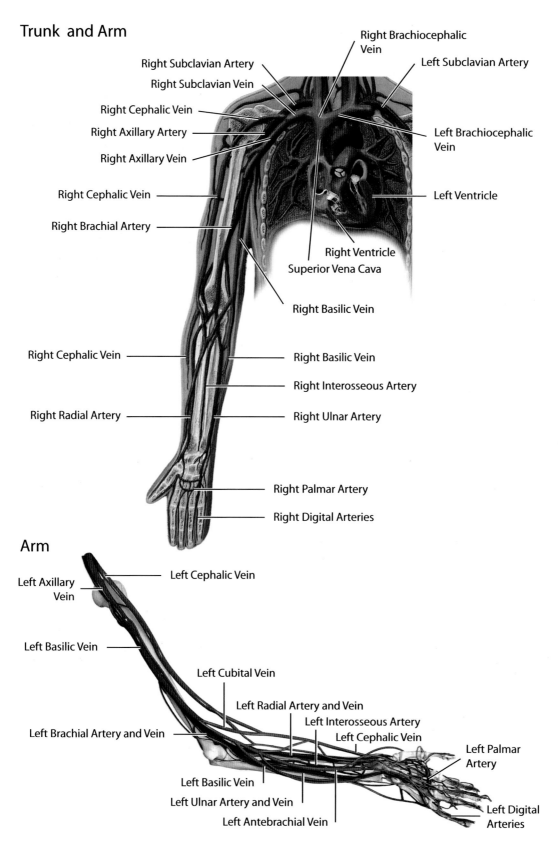

Right Brachiocephalic Vein

Right Subclavian Artery

Left Subclavian Artery

Right Subclavian Vein

Right Cephalic Vein

Right Axillary Artery

Left Brachiocephalic Vein

Right Axillary Vein

Right Cephalic Vein

Left Ventricle

Right Brachial Artery

Right Ventricle

Superior Vena Cava

Right Basilic Vein

Right Cephalic Vein

Right Basilic Vein

Right Interosseous Artery

Right Radial Artery

Right Ulnar Artery

Right Palmar Artery

Right Digital Arteries

Arm

Left Axillary Vein

Left Cephalic Vein

Left Basilic Vein

Left Cubital Vein

Left Radial Artery and Vein

Left Interosseous Artery

Left Brachial Artery and Vein

Left Cephalic Vein

Left Palmar Artery

Left Basilic Vein

Left Ulnar Artery and Vein

Left Antebrachial Vein

Left Digital Arteries

Arteries and Veins - Abdomen and Pelvis

Abdomen and Pelvis

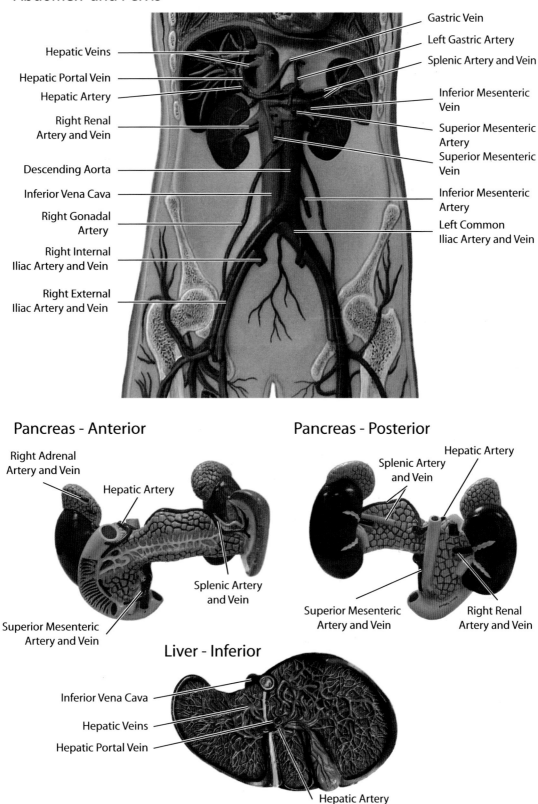

Hepatic Veins

Hepatic Portal Vein

Hepatic Artery

Right Renal
Artery and Vein

Descending Aorta

Inferior Vena Cava

Right Gonadal
Artery

Right Internal
Iliac Artery and Vein

Right External
Iliac Artery and Vein

Gastric Vein

Left Gastric Artery

Splenic Artery and Vein

Inferior Mesenteric
Vein

Superior Mesenteric
Artery

Superior Mesenteric
Vein

Inferior Mesenteric
Artery

Left Common
Iliac Artery and Vein

Pancreas - Anterior

Right Adrenal
Artery and Vein

Hepatic Artery

Splenic Artery
and Vein

Superior Mesenteric
Artery and Vein

Pancreas - Posterior

Hepatic Artery

Splenic Artery
and Vein

Superior Mesenteric
Artery and Vein

Right Renal
Artery and Vein

Liver - Inferior

Inferior Vena Cava

Hepatic Veins

Hepatic Portal Vein

Hepatic Artery

Arteries and Veins - Pelvis, Thigh and Leg

Pelvis, Thigh and Leg

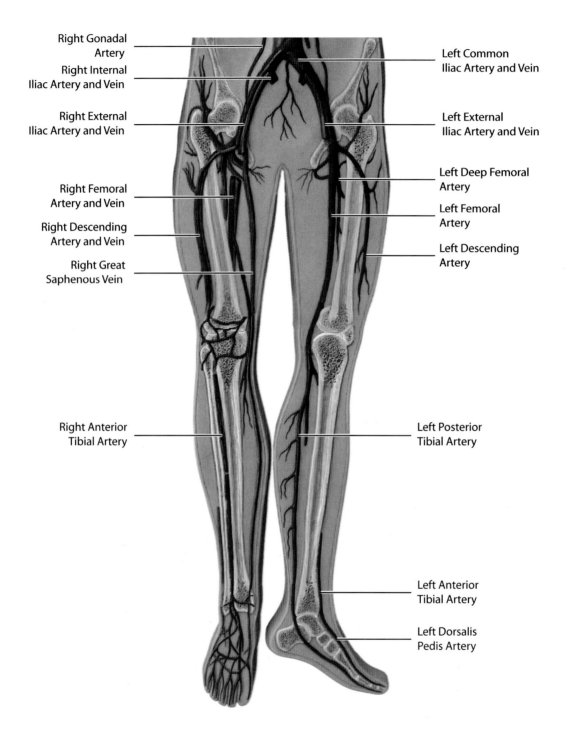

Right Gonadal Artery

Right Internal Iliac Artery and Vein

Right External Iliac Artery and Vein

Right Femoral Artery and Vein

Right Descending Artery and Vein

Right Great Saphenous Vein

Right Anterior Tibial Artery

Left Common Iliac Artery and Vein

Left External Iliac Artery and Vein

Left Deep Femoral Artery

Left Femoral Artery

Left Descending Artery

Left Posterior Tibial Artery

Left Anterior Tibial Artery

Left Dorsalis Pedis Artery

Arteries, Capillaries and Veins - Histology

Vein and Artery

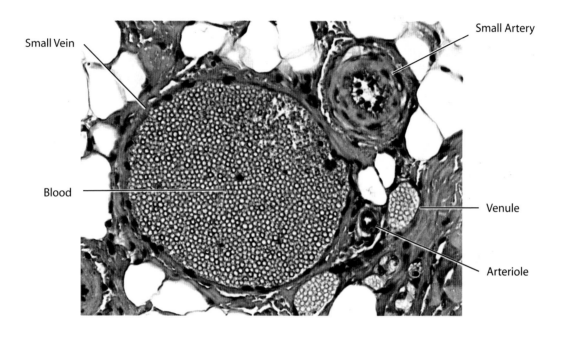

Small Vein

Small Artery

Blood

Venule

Arteriole

Arteries, Capillaries and Veins

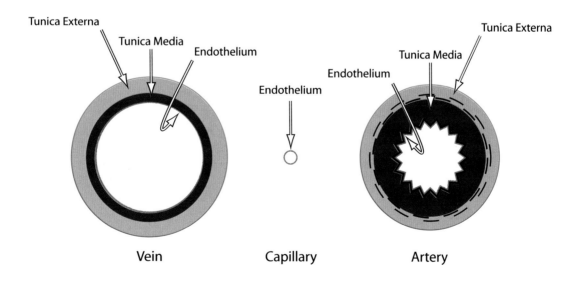

Tunica Externa

Tunica Media

Endothelium

Endothelium

Tunica Externa

Tunica Media

Endothelium

Vein

Capillary

Artery

Arteries, Veins and Smooth Muscle - Histology

Artery and Vein

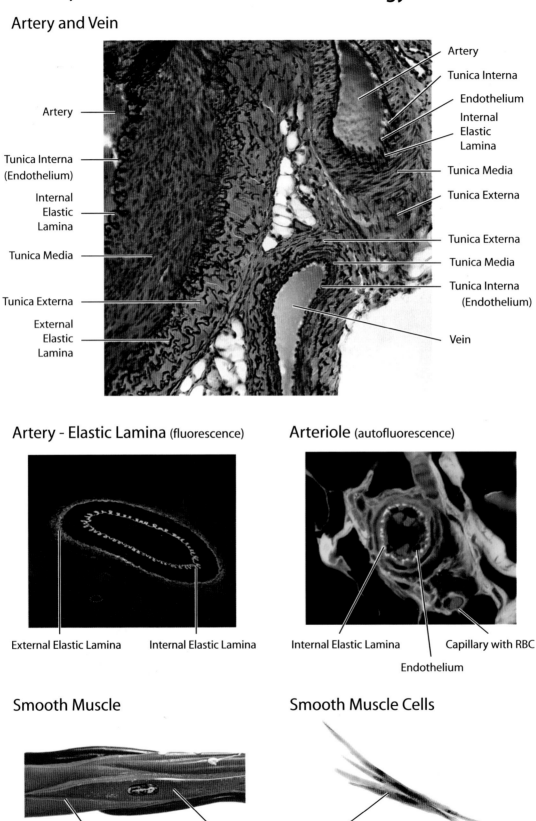

Artery

Tunica Interna (Endothelium)

Internal Elastic Lamina

Tunica Media

Tunica Externa

External Elastic Lamina

Artery

Tunica Interna

Endothelium

Internal Elastic Lamina

Tunica Media

Tunica Externa

Tunica Externa

Tunica Media

Tunica Interna (Endothelium)

Vein

Artery - Elastic Lamina (fluorescence)

External Elastic Lamina   Internal Elastic Lamina

Arteriole (autofluorescence)

Internal Elastic Lamina   Capillary with RBC

Endothelium

Smooth Muscle

Endomysium   Smooth Muscle Cell

Smooth Muscle Cells

Smooth Muscle Cells

Microcirculation and Endothelial Cells

Microcirculation

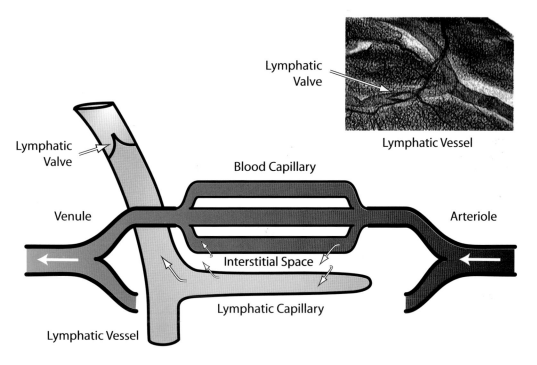

Lymphatic Valve

Lymphatic Vessel

Lymphatic Valve

Blood Capillary

Venule

Arteriole

Interstitial Space

Lymphatic Capillary

Lymphatic Vessel

Capillary permeability

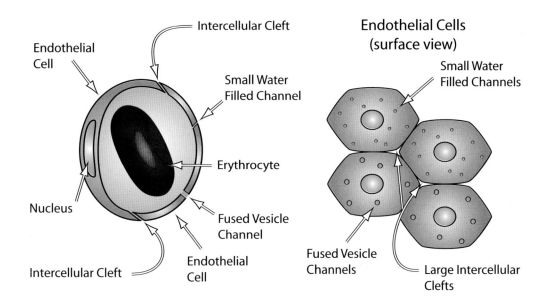

Intercellular Cleft

Endothelial Cell

Small Water Filled Channel

Erythrocyte

Nucleus

Fused Vesicle Channel

Intercellular Cleft

Endothelial Cell

Endothelial Cells (surface view)

Small Water Filled Channels

Fused Vesicle Channels

Large Intercellular Clefts

Blood

Blood Composition

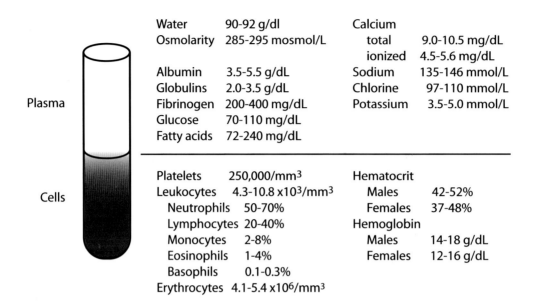

Water	90-92 g/dl	Calcium		
Osmolarity	285-295 mosmol/L	total	9.0-10.5 mg/dL	
		ionized	4.5-5.6 mg/dL	
Albumin	3.5-5.5 g/dL	Sodium	135-146 mmol/L	
Globulins	2.0-3.5 g/dL	Chlorine	97-110 mmol/L	
Fibrinogen	200-400 mg/dL	Potassium	3.5-5.0 mmol/L	
Glucose	70-110 mg/dL			
Fatty acids	72-240 mg/dL			

Plasma

Cells

Platelets	250,000/mm^3	Hematocrit	
Leukocytes	4.3-10.8 x10^3/mm^3	Males	42-52%
Neutrophils	50-70%	Females	37-48%
Lymphocytes	20-40%	Hemoglobin	
Monocytes	2-8%	Males	14-18 g/dL
Eosinophils	1-4%	Females	12-16 g/dL
Basophils	0.1-0.3%		
Erythrocytes	4.1-5.4 x10^6/mm^3		

Blood Cells

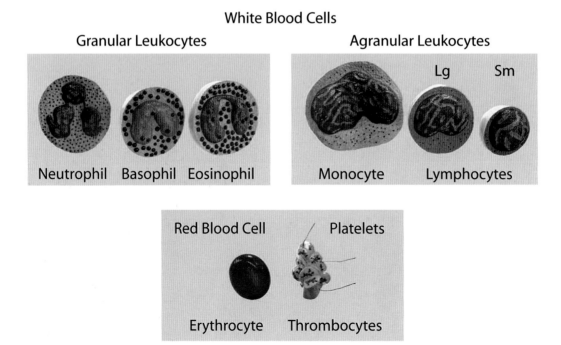

White Blood Cells

Granular Leukocytes

Neutrophil   Basophil   Eosinophil

Agranular Leukocytes

Lg   Sm

Monocyte   Lymphocytes

Red Blood Cell   Platelets

Erythrocyte   Thrombocytes

Blood - Histology

Erythrocytes and Platelets

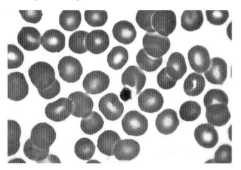

Neutrophil

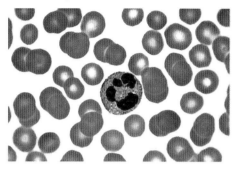

Small Lymphocyte

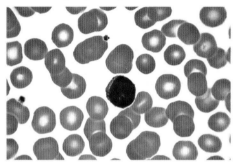

Large Lymphocyte

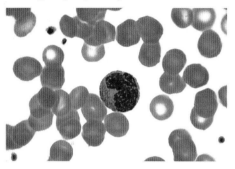

Monocyte

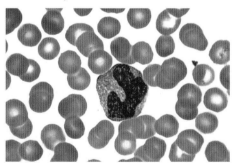

Eosinophil

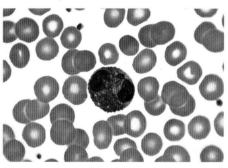

Basophil

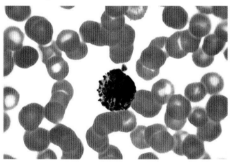

Erythrocytes and Platelets

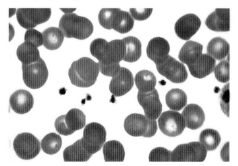

Section 6

Airways and Lungs, GI Tract, Kidneys and Bladder

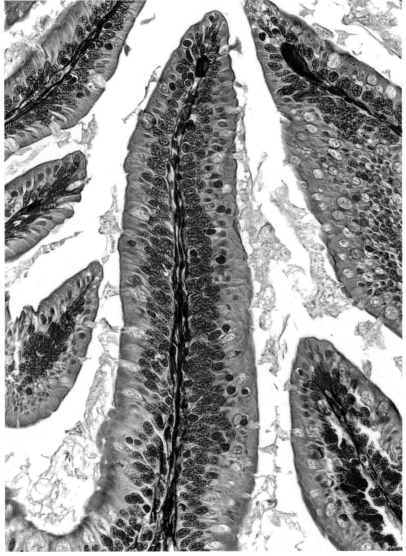

Intestinal villi showing goblet cells (brightfield, trichrome; x350)

Nose and Throat

Nose and Throat

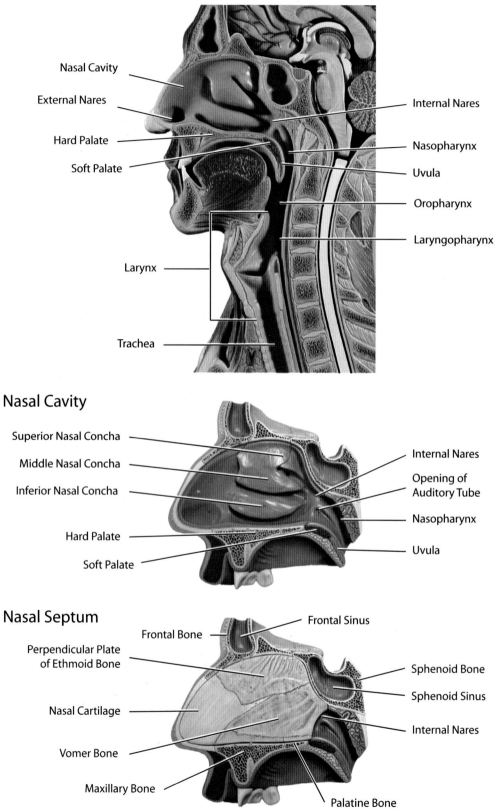

Nasal Cavity

External Nares

Hard Palate

Soft Palate

Internal Nares

Nasopharynx

Uvula

Oropharynx

Laryngopharynx

Larynx

Trachea

Nasal Cavity

Superior Nasal Concha

Middle Nasal Concha

Inferior Nasal Concha

Hard Palate

Soft Palate

Internal Nares

Opening of Auditory Tube

Nasopharynx

Uvula

Nasal Septum

Frontal Sinus

Frontal Bone

Perpendicular Plate of Ethmoid Bone

Nasal Cartilage

Vomer Bone

Maxillary Bone

Sphenoid Bone

Sphenoid Sinus

Internal Nares

Palatine Bone

Larynx, Trachea and Bronchi - with Histology

Larynx, Trachea and Bronchi

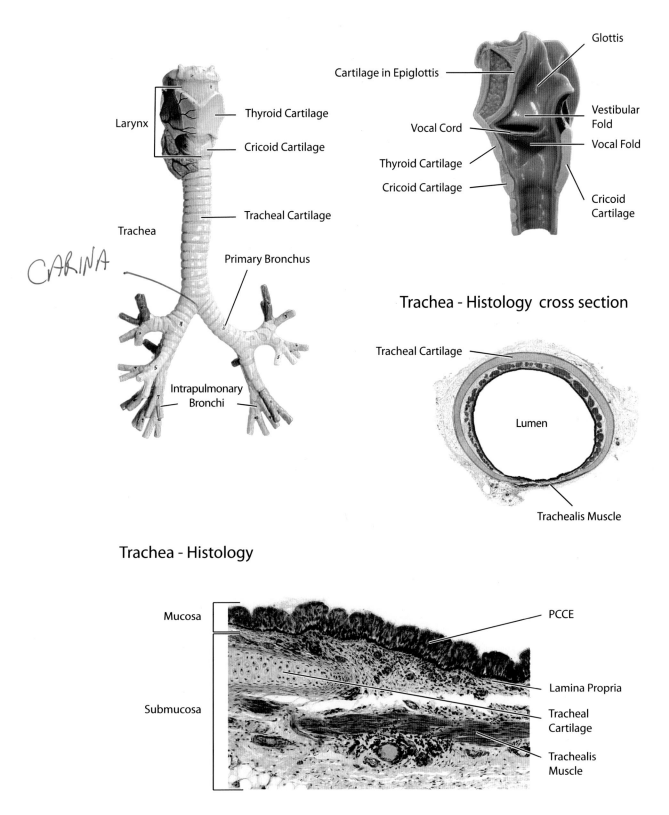

Larynx

Thyroid Cartilage

Cricoid Cartilage

Trachea

CARINA

Tracheal Cartilage

Primary Bronchus

Intrapulmonary Bronchi

Larynx - Midsagittal

Cartilage in Epiglottis

Glottis

Vocal Cord

Vestibular Fold

Thyroid Cartilage

Vocal Fold

Cricoid Cartilage

Cricoid Cartilage

Trachea - Histology cross section

Tracheal Cartilage

Lumen

Trachealis Muscle

Trachea - Histology

Mucosa

PCCE

Lamina Propria

Submucosa

Tracheal Cartilage

Trachealis Muscle

Pleural Cavities, Lungs and Pleural Membranes

Pleural Cavities and Lungs

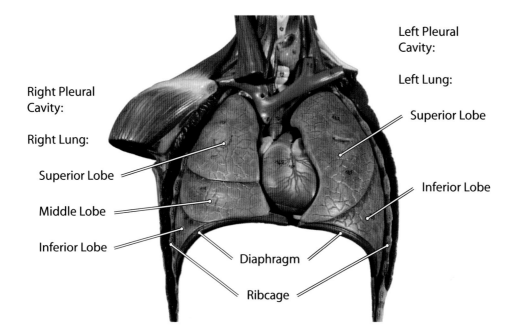

Left Pleural Cavity:

Left Lung:

Right Pleural Cavity:

Right Lung:

Superior Lobe

Superior Lobe

Middle Lobe

Inferior Lobe

Inferior Lobe

Diaphragm

Ribcage

Pleural Membranes

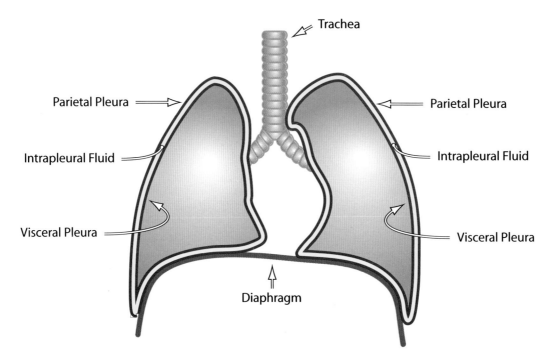

Trachea

Parietal Pleura

Parietal Pleura

Intrapleural Fluid

Intrapleural Fluid

Visceral Pleura

Visceral Pleura

Diaphragm

Alveolar Sacs and Alveoli

Alveolar Sacs

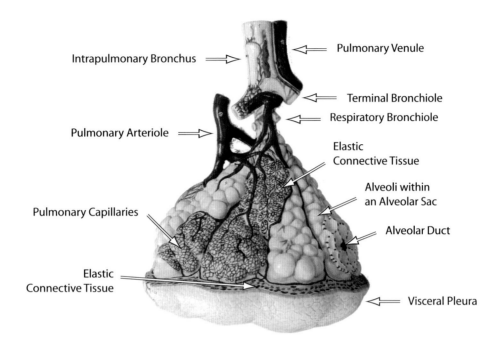

Intrapulmonary Bronchus

Pulmonary Venule

Terminal Bronchiole

Respiratory Bronchiole

Pulmonary Arteriole

Elastic Connective Tissue

Alveoli within an Alveolar Sac

Pulmonary Capillaries

Alveolar Duct

Elastic Connective Tissue

Visceral Pleura

Alveoli

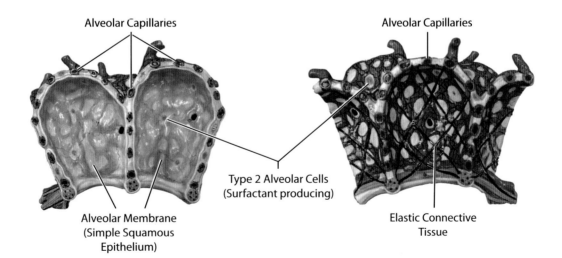

Alveolar Capillaries

Alveolar Capillaries

Type 2 Alveolar Cells (Surfactant producing)

Alveolar Membrane (Simple Squamous Epithelium)

Elastic Connective Tissue

Intrapulmonary Bronchi - Histology

Artery and Bronchus

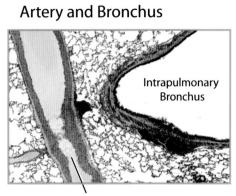

Intrapulmonary Bronchus

Intrapulmonary Artery

Intrapulmonary Bronchus

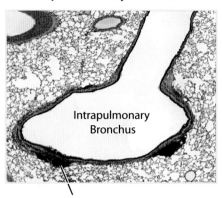

Intrapulmonary Bronchus

Lymphatic Nodules

Lung - overview

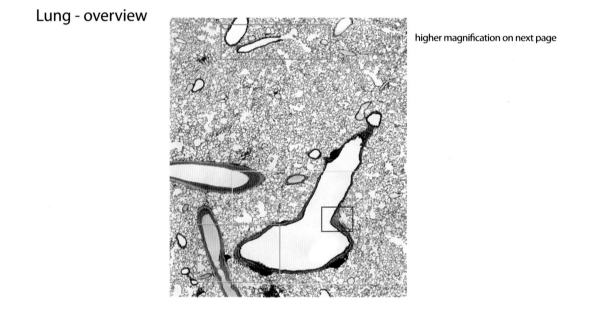

higher magnification on next page

Mucosa and Submucosa

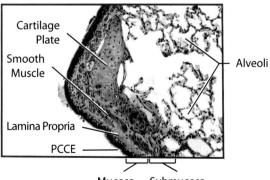

Cartilage Plate

Smooth Muscle

Lamina Propria

PCCE

Alveoli

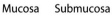

Mucosa   Submucosa

PCCE

Cilia

Bronchioles and Alveoli - Histology

Terminal Bronchiole

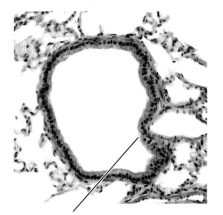

Cuboidal-like Epithelium

Smoke - Terminal Bronchiole

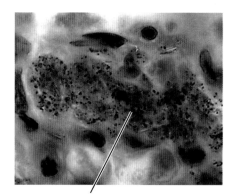

Smoke on surface of Epithelium

Terminal and Respiratory Bronchioles and Alveolar Ducts
(refer to previous page for reference image)

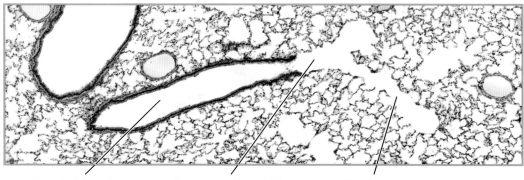

Terminal Bronchiole   Respiratory Bronchiole   Alveolar Duct

Respiratory Bronchiole and Alveoli

Alveoli

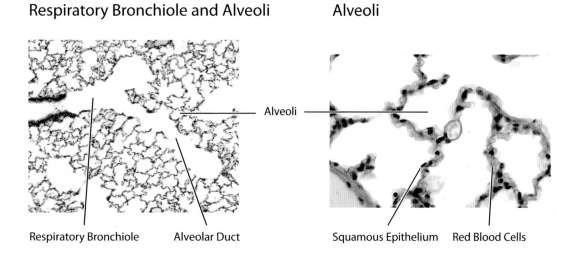

Respiratory Bronchiole   Alveolar Duct

Alveoli

Squamous Epithelium   Red Blood Cells

Mouth, Esophagus and Teeth

Mouth and Esophagus

Mechanical Digestion: Chewing

Chemical Digestion:
1) Salivary (parotid) amylase starts the breakdown of carbohydrates to disaccharides.
2) Salivary (sublingual) lipase starts the breakdown of fats to fatty acids.

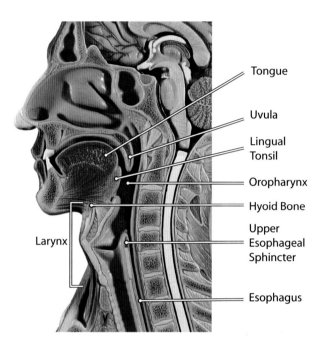

Tongue

Uvula

Lingual Tonsil

Oropharynx

Hyoid Bone

Upper Esophageal Sphincter

Esophagus

Larynx

Tooth

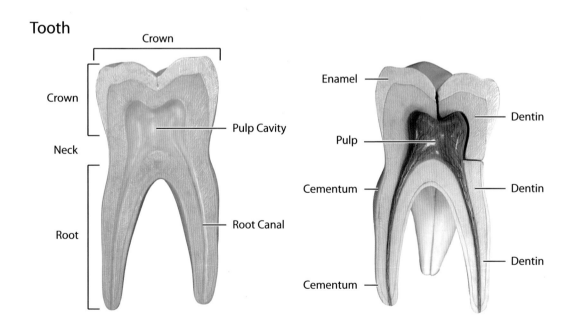

Crown

Crown

Neck

Root

Pulp Cavity

Root Canal

Enamel

Pulp

Cementum

Cementum

Dentin

Dentin

Dentin

Jaw and Teeth

Lower Jaw - Lateral

Central Incisor
Cuspid
2nd Premolar
2nd Molar
1st Molar
1st Premolar
Lateral Incisor

Lower Jaw - Mesial

Central Incisor
Cuspid
2nd Premolar
2nd Molar
Inferior Alveolar nerve
Mandibular Foramen
1st Molar
1st Premolar
Lateral Incisor

Upper and Lower Jaw - Lateral

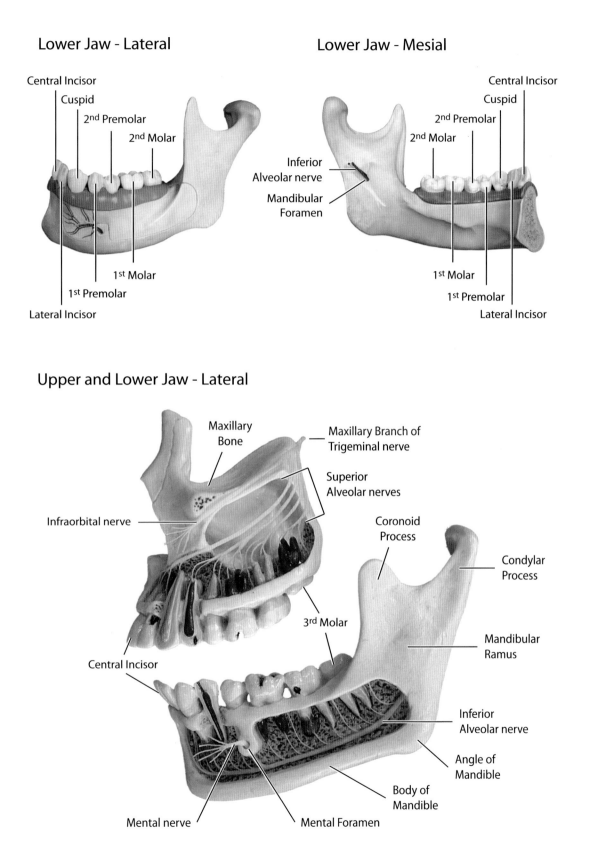

Maxillary Bone
Maxillary Branch of Trigeminal nerve
Superior Alveolar nerves
Infraorbital nerve
Coronoid Process
Condylar Process
3rd Molar
Central Incisor
Mandibular Ramus
Inferior Alveolar nerve
Angle of Mandible
Body of Mandible
Mental nerve
Mental Foramen

Stomach

Abdominal Cavity

Stomach

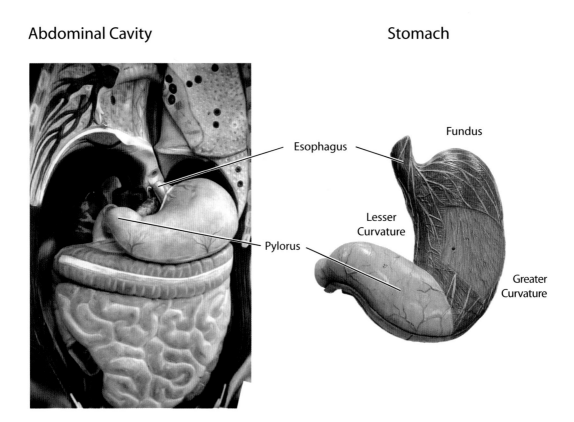

Esophagus

Pylorus

Fundus

Lesser Curvature

Greater Curvature

Stomach

Mechanical Digestion: Churning

Chemical Digestion:
1) Hydrochloric acid starts the hydrolysis of many proteins.
2) Hydrochloric acid converts pepsinogen to gastric pepsin.
3) Gastric pepsin starts the breakdown of proteins to polypeptides and peptides.

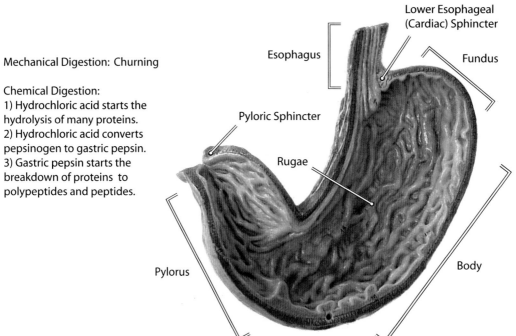

Lower Esophageal (Cardiac) Sphincter

Esophagus

Fundus

Pyloric Sphincter

Rugae

Pylorus

Body

Small and Large Intestines

Intestines

Mechanical Digestion: Segmentation

Chemical Digestion:
1) Pancreatic amylase continues the breakdown of carbohydrates to disaccharides.
2) Intestinal disaccharidases break down the disaccharides to monosaccharides.
3) Pancreatic proteinases continue the breakdown of proteins to polypeptides and peptides.
4) Pancreatic and intestinal peptidases break down the peptides to amino acids.
5) Liver bile emulsifies fats.
6) Pancreatic lipases break down fats to fatty acids and monoglycerides.

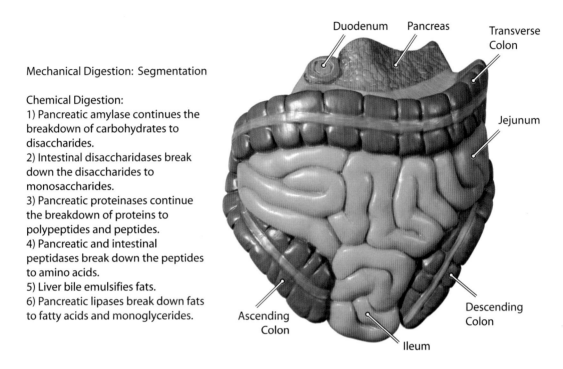

Intestine - Posterior

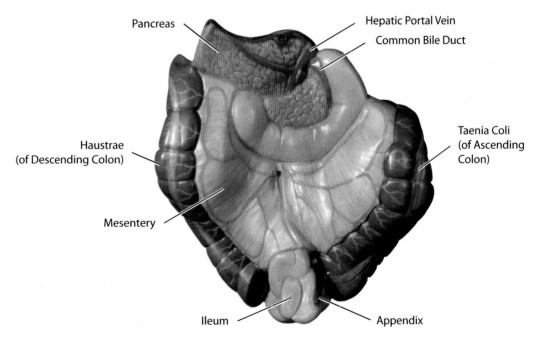

Large Intestines

Large Intestines (Colon)

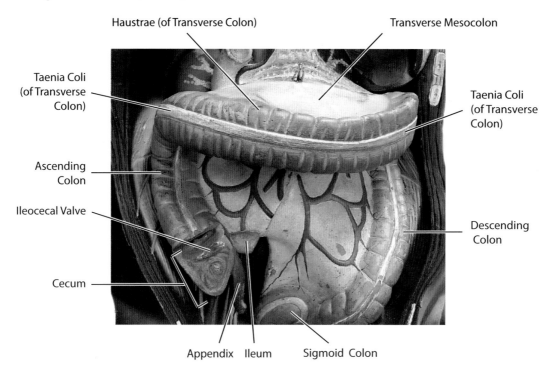

Haustrae (of Transverse Colon)

Transverse Mesocolon

Taenia Coli (of Transverse Colon)

Taenia Coli (of Transverse Colon)

Ascending Colon

Ileocecal Valve

Descending Colon

Cecum

Appendix   Ileum   Sigmoid Colon

Rectum and Anus

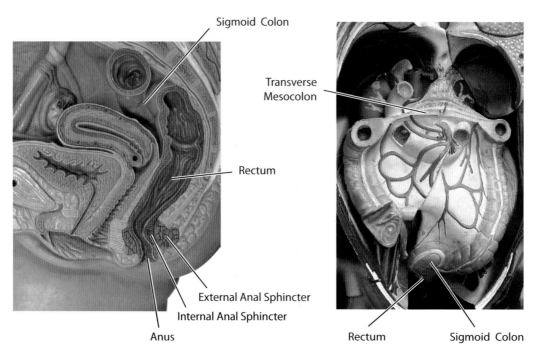

Sigmoid Colon

Transverse Mesocolon

Rectum

External Anal Sphincter

Internal Anal Sphincter

Anus

Rectum   Sigmoid Colon

Liver and Pancreas

Liver

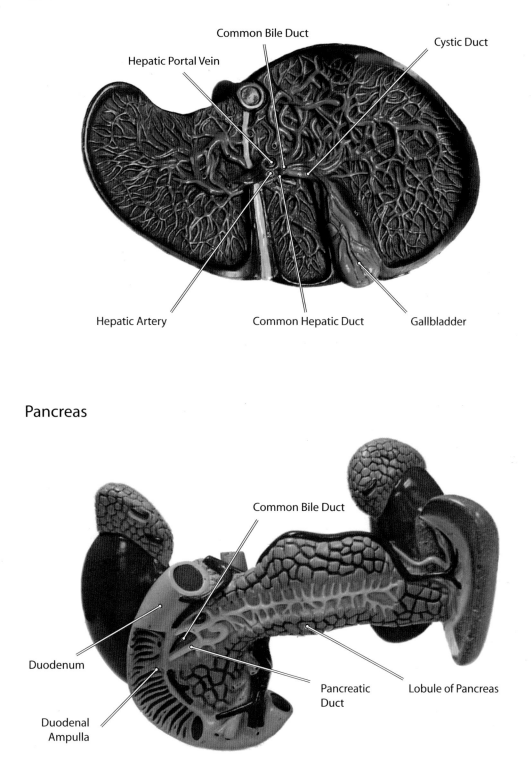

Common Bile Duct

Hepatic Portal Vein

Cystic Duct

Hepatic Artery

Common Hepatic Duct

Gallbladder

Pancreas

Common Bile Duct

Duodenum

Duodenal Ampulla

Pancreatic Duct

Lobule of Pancreas

Esophagus - Histology

Esophagus

Esophagus (autofluorescence)

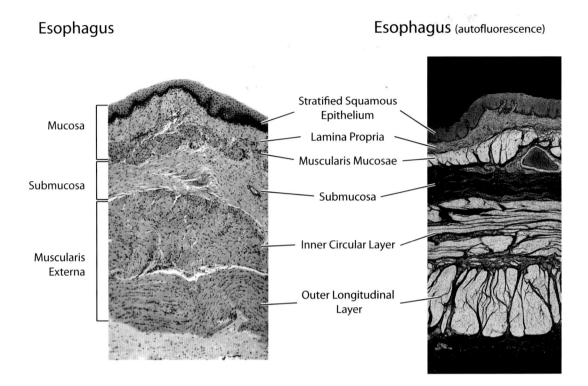

Mucosa

Submucosa

Muscularis Externa

Stratified Squamous Epithelium

Lamina Propria

Muscularis Mucosae

Submucosa

Inner Circular Layer

Outer Longitudinal Layer

Esophagus

Epithelium (autofluorescence)

Mucosa

Submucosa

Muscularis Externa

Stratified Squamous Epithelium

Lamina Propria

Muscularis Mucosae

Submucosa

Inner Circular Layer

Outer Longitudinal Layer

Non-Keratinized
Stratified Squamous Epithelium

Stomach - Histology

Wall of Stomach

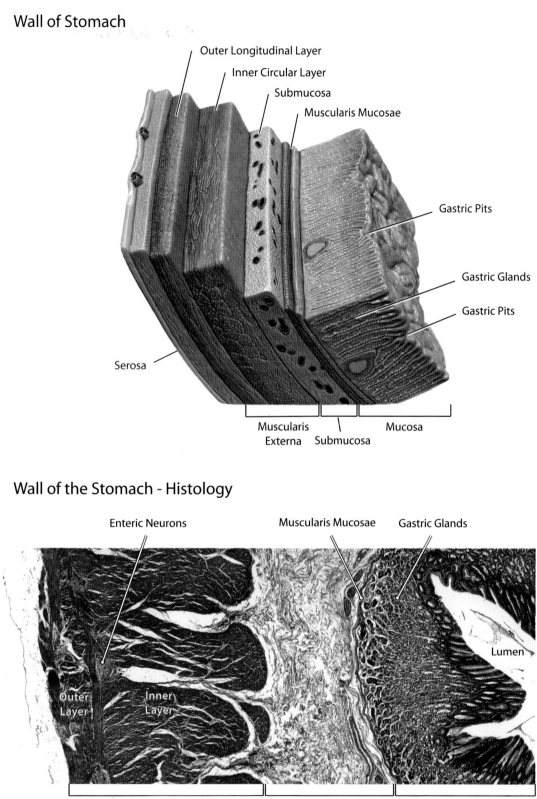

Outer Longitudinal Layer

Inner Circular Layer

Submucosa

Muscularis Mucosae

Gastric Pits

Gastric Glands

Gastric Pits

Serosa

Muscularis Externa

Submucosa

Mucosa

Wall of the Stomach - Histology

Enteric Neurons

Muscularis Mucosae

Gastric Glands

Lumen

Outer Layer

Inner Layer

Muscularis Externa

Submucosa

Mucosa

Stomach and Intestines - Histology

Mucosa of the Stomach - Histology

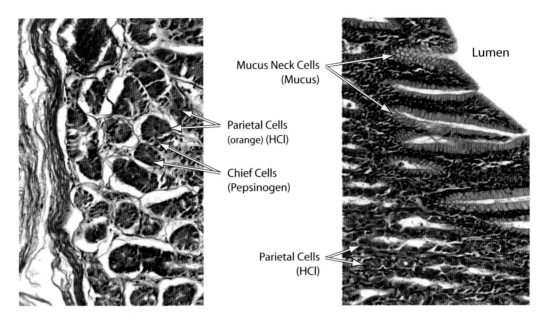

Mucus Neck Cells
(Mucus)

Lumen

Parietal Cells
(orange) (HCl)

Chief Cells
(Pepsinogen)

Parietal Cells
(HCl)

x400

x200

Small Intestines

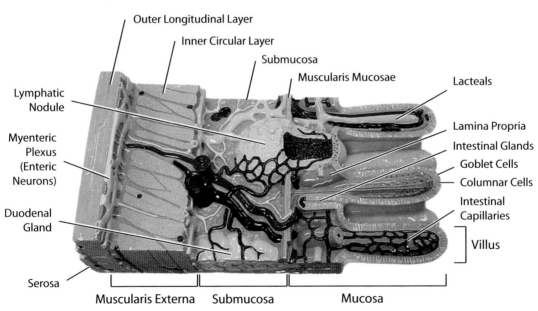

Outer Longitudinal Layer

Inner Circular Layer

Submucosa

Muscularis Mucosae

Lacteals

Lymphatic
Nodule

Lamina Propria

Intestinal Glands

Myenteric
Plexus
(Enteric
Neurons)

Goblet Cells

Columnar Cells

Intestinal
Capillaries

Duodenal
Gland

Villus

Serosa

Muscularis Externa   Submucosa   Mucosa

Duodenum - Histology

Wall of the Duodenum

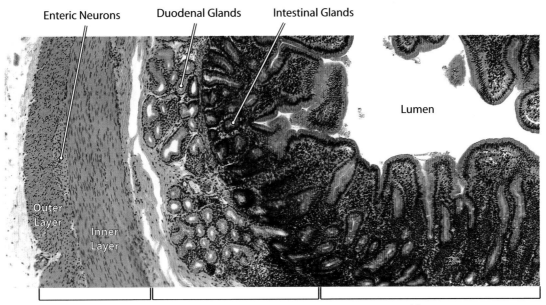

Enteric Neurons   Duodenal Glands   Intestinal Glands

Lumen

Outer Layer

Inner Layer

Muscularis Externa   Submucosa   Mucosa

Duodenum

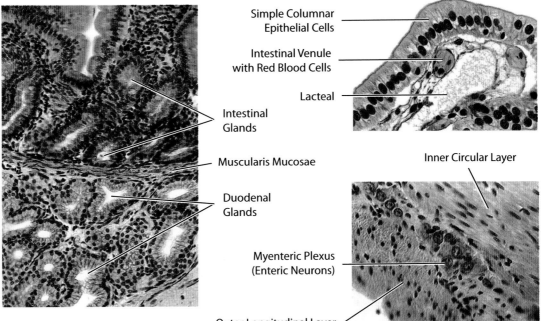

Simple Columnar Epithelial Cells

Intestinal Venule with Red Blood Cells

Lacteal

Intestinal Glands

Muscularis Mucosae

Duodenal Glands

Inner Circular Layer

Myenteric Plexus (Enteric Neurons)

Outer Longitudinal Layer

Liver and Pancreas - Histology

Liver Lobules

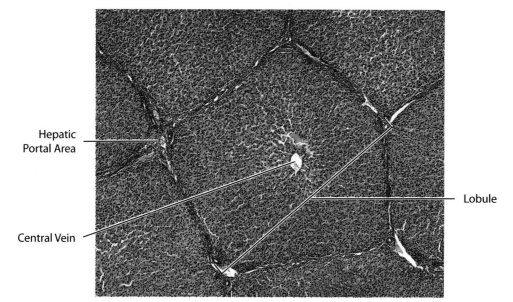

Hepatic Portal Area

Central Vein

Lobule

Hepatic Portal Area

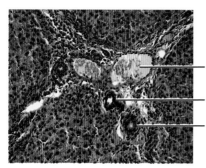

Hepatic Portal Venule

Arteriole

Bile Ductule

Central Canal in Liver

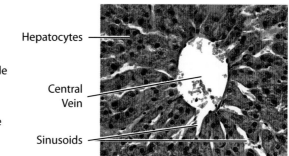

Hepatocytes

Central Vein

Sinusoids

Pancreatic Lobules

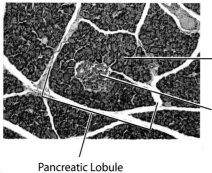

Pancreatic Islet

Pancreatic Lobule

Pancreatic Acini

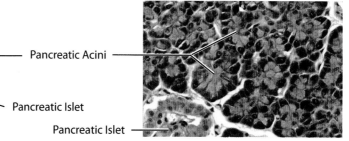

Pancreatic Acini

Pancreatic Islet

Urinary Tract and Kidney

Urinary Tract

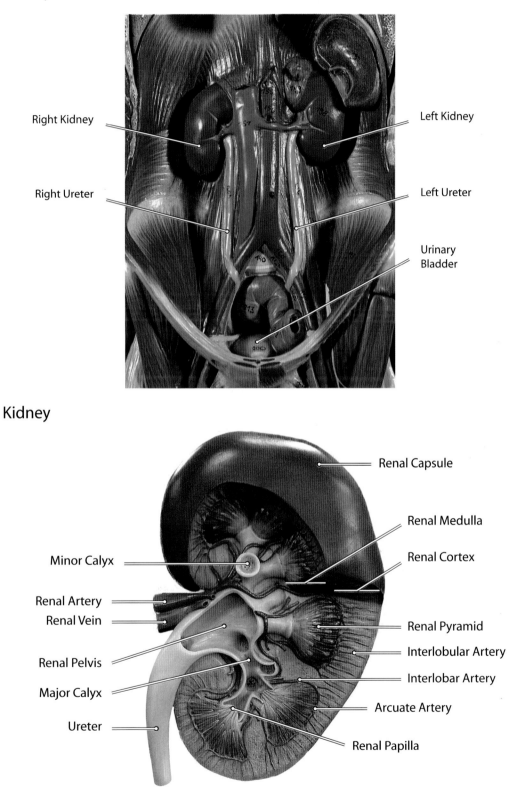

Right Kidney

Left Kidney

Right Ureter

Left Ureter

Urinary
Bladder

Kidney

Renal Capsule

Renal Medulla

Renal Cortex

Minor Calyx

Renal Artery

Renal Vein

Renal Pyramid

Interlobular Artery

Renal Pelvis

Interlobar Artery

Major Calyx

Arcuate Artery

Ureter

Renal Papilla

Nephron and Renal Corpuscle

Nephron

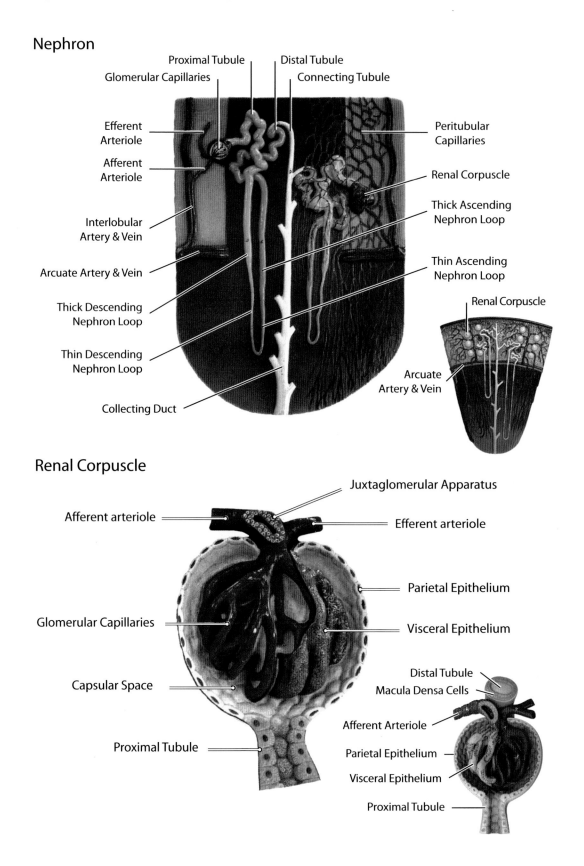

Proximal Tubule

Glomerular Capillaries

Distal Tubule

Connecting Tubule

Efferent
Arteriole

Afferent
Arteriole

Interlobular
Artery & Vein

Arcuate Artery & Vein

Thick Descending
Nephron Loop

Thin Descending
Nephron Loop

Collecting Duct

Peritubular
Capillaries

Renal Corpuscle

Thick Ascending
Nephron Loop

Thin Ascending
Nephron Loop

Renal Corpuscle

Arcuate
Artery & Vein

Renal Corpuscle

Juxtaglomerular Apparatus

Afferent arteriole

Efferent arteriole

Glomerular Capillaries

Parietal Epithelium

Visceral Epithelium

Capsular Space

Distal Tubule

Macula Densa Cells

Afferent Arteriole

Parietal Epithelium

Proximal Tubule

Visceral Epithelium

Proximal Tubule

Nephron and Renal Corpuscle

Reabsorption in Tubules and Ducts

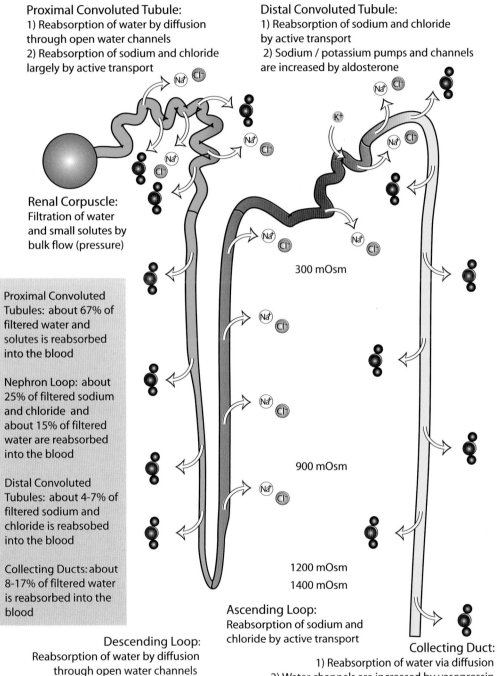

Proximal Convoluted Tubule:
1) Reabsorption of water by diffusion through open water channels
2) Reabsorption of sodium and chloride largely by active transport

Distal Convoluted Tubule:
1) Reabsorption of sodium and chloride by active transport
2) Sodium / potassium pumps and channels are increased by aldosterone

Renal Corpuscle:
Filtration of water and small solutes by bulk flow (pressure)

Proximal Convoluted Tubules: about 67% of filtered water and solutes is reabsorbed into the blood

Nephron Loop: about 25% of filtered sodium and chloride and about 15% of filtered water are reabsorbed into the blood

Distal Convoluted Tubules: about 4-7% of filtered sodium and chloride is reabsobed into the blood

Collecting Ducts: about 8-17% of filtered water is reabsorbed into the blood

300 mOsm

900 mOsm

1200 mOsm
1400 mOsm

Descending Loop:
Reabsorption of water by diffusion through open water channels

Ascending Loop:
Reabsorption of sodium and chloride by active transport

Collecting Duct:
1) Reabsorption of water via diffusion
2) Water channels are increased by vasopressin

Renal Corpuscles and Ureter - Histology

Renal Corpuscle

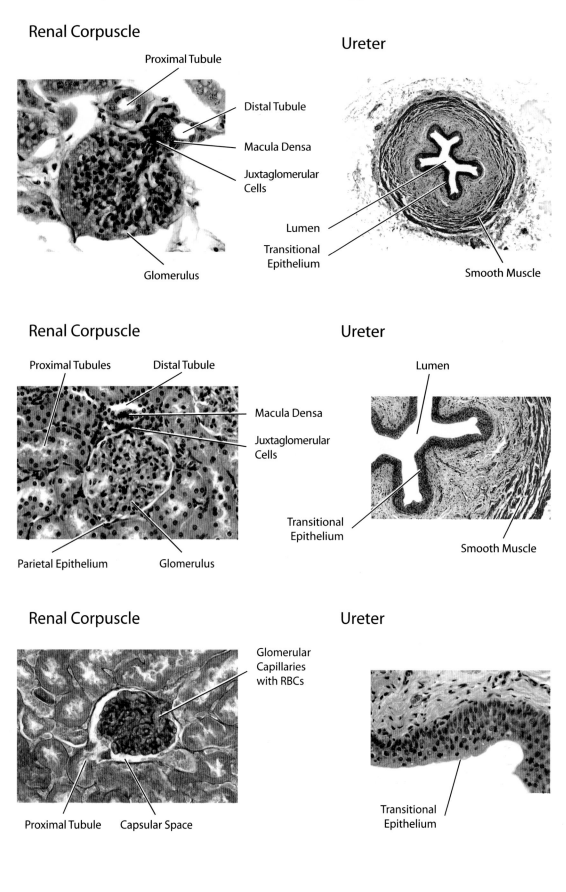

Proximal Tubule

Distal Tubule

Macula Densa

Juxtaglomerular Cells

Glomerulus

Ureter

Lumen

Transitional Epithelium

Smooth Muscle

Renal Corpuscle

Proximal Tubules

Distal Tubule

Macula Densa

Juxtaglomerular Cells

Parietal Epithelium

Glomerulus

Ureter

Lumen

Transitional Epithelium

Smooth Muscle

Renal Corpuscle

Glomerular Capillaries with RBCs

Proximal Tubule

Capsular Space

Ureter

Transitional Epithelium

Section 7

Autonomic Nervous System, Endocrine Glands, and Reproductive Organs

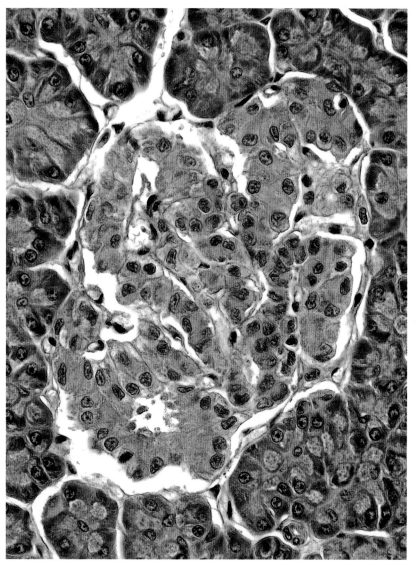

Pancreas showing pancreatic islet (brightfield, H&E; x430)

Parasympathetic Nervous System

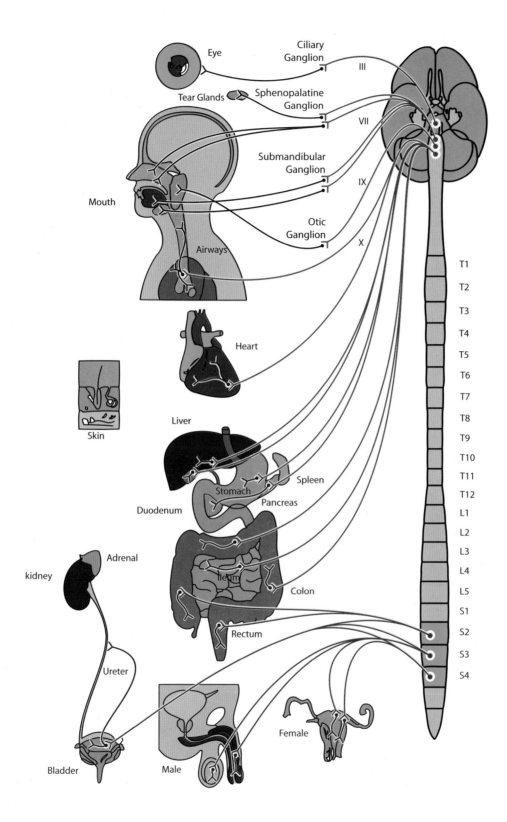

Eye	Ciliary Ganglion
	III
Tear Glands	Sphenopalatine Ganglion
	VII
Mouth	Submandibular Ganglion
	IX
	Otic Ganglion
Airways	X
	T1
	T2
Heart	T3
	T4
	T5
	T6
Skin	T7
	T8
Liver	T9
	T10
	T11
Spleen	T12
Stomach	L1
Duodenum	Pancreas
	L2
	L3
Adrenal	L4
kidney	Ileum
	L5
	Colon
	S1
Rectum	S2
Ureter	S3
	S4
	Female
Bladder	
Male	

Parasympathetic Ganglia and Neurotransmitters

Parasympathetic Ganglia

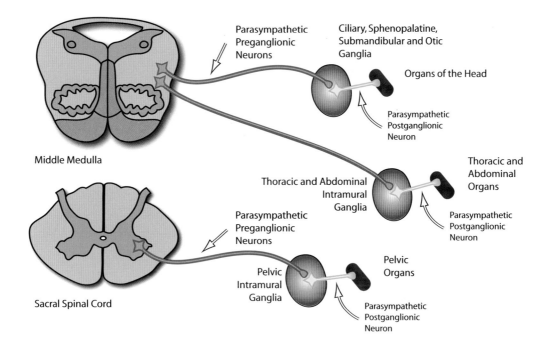

Parasympathetic Neurotransmitters

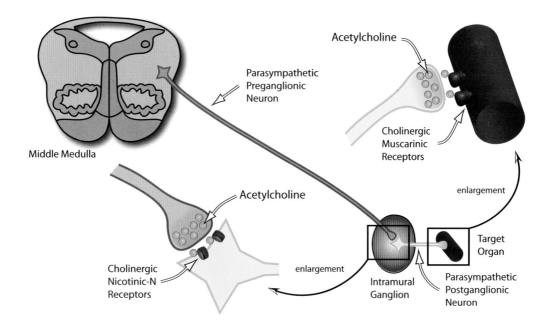

Sympathetic Nervous System

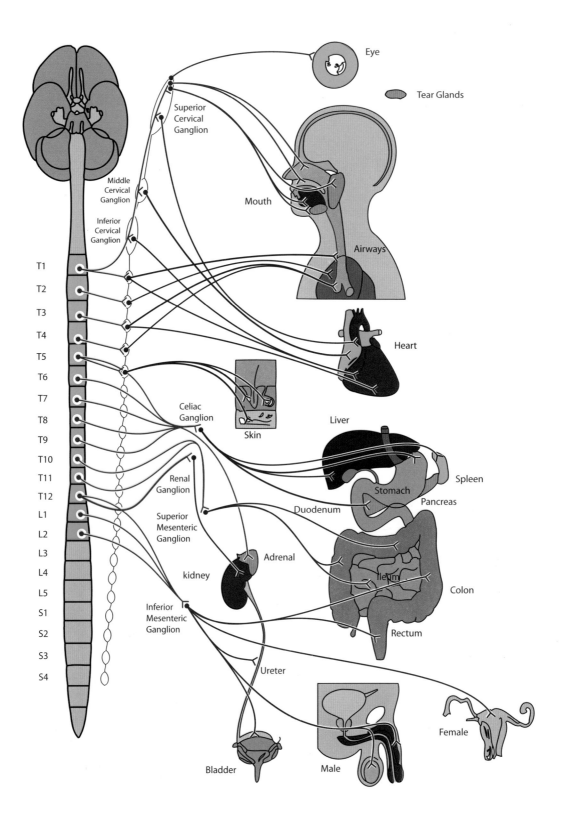

Eye

Tear Glands

Superior Cervical Ganglion

Middle Cervical Ganglion

Inferior Cervical Ganglion

Mouth

Airways

Heart

Celiac Ganglion

Skin

Liver

Spleen

Stomach

Pancreas

Duodenum

Renal Ganglion

Superior Mesenteric Ganglion

kidney

Adrenal

Ileum

Colon

Inferior Mesenteric Ganglion

Rectum

Ureter

Bladder

Male

Female

T1
T2
T3
T4
T5
T6
T7
T8
T9
T10
T11
T12
L1
L2
L3
L4
L5
S1
S2
S3
S4

Sympathetic Ganglia and Neurotransmitters

Sympathetic Ganglia

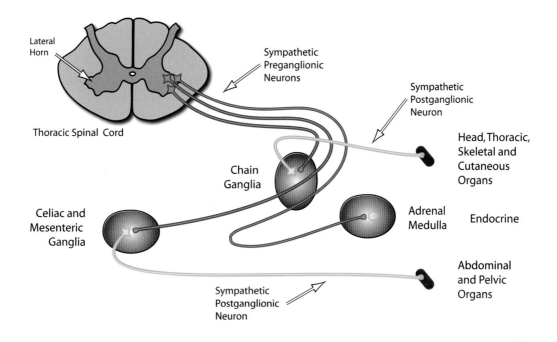

Sympathetic Neurotransmitters

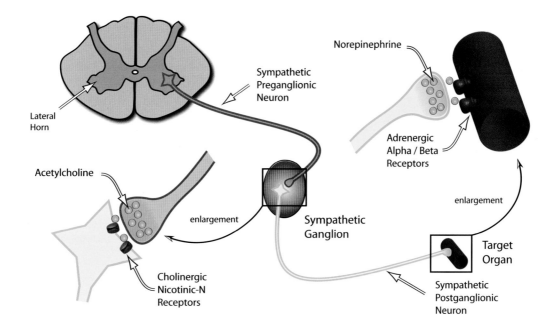

Sympathetic Chain Ganglia

Chain Ganglia

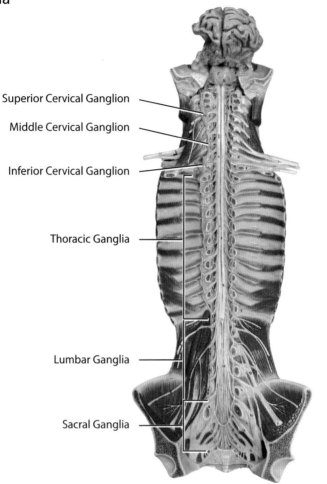

Superior Cervical Ganglion

Middle Cervical Ganglion

Inferior Cervical Ganglion

Thoracic Ganglia

Lumbar Ganglia

Sacral Ganglia

Chain Ganglia

Thoracic Chain Ganglia

Gray Ramus

White Ramus

Gray Ramus

Thoracic Spinal Nerve

White Ramus

Splanchnic Nerves

Anterior Roots

Rami Communicans

Autonomic Nervous System

Sympathetic
- Yellow nerves

Parasympathetic
- White nerves

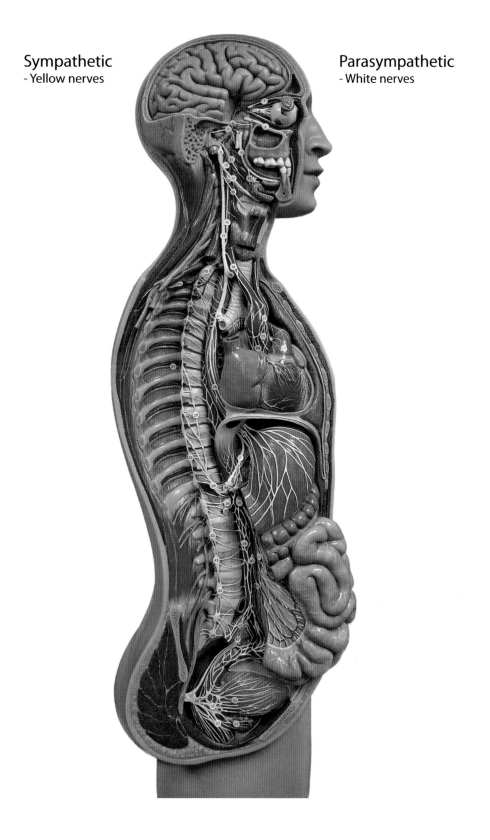

Overview of Endocrine Glands

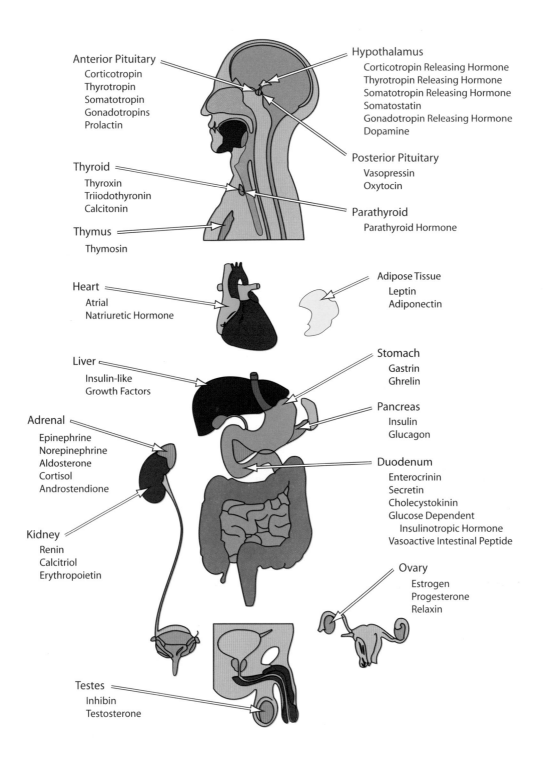

Anterior Pituitary
Corticotropin
Thyrotropin
Somatotropin
Gonadotropins
Prolactin

Hypothalamus
Corticotropin Releasing Hormone
Thyrotropin Releasing Hormone
Somatotropin Releasing Hormone
Somatostatin
Gonadotropin Releasing Hormone
Dopamine

Posterior Pituitary
Vasopressin
Oxytocin

Thyroid
Thyroxin
Triiodothyronin
Calcitonin

Parathyroid
Parathyroid Hormone

Thymus
Thymosin

Heart
Atrial
Natriuretic Hormone

Adipose Tissue
Leptin
Adiponectin

Liver
Insulin-like
Growth Factors

Stomach
Gastrin
Ghrelin

Pancreas
Insulin
Glucagon

Adrenal
Epinephrine
Norepinephrine
Aldosterone
Cortisol
Androstendione

Duodenum
Enterocrinin
Secretin
Cholecystokinin
Glucose Dependent
   Insulinotropic Hormone
Vasoactive Intestinal Peptide

Kidney
Renin
Calcitriol
Erythropoietin

Ovary
Estrogen
Progesterone
Relaxin

Testes
Inhibin
Testosterone

Endocrine Glands

Pituitary and Thyroid Glands

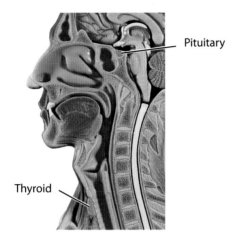

Pituitary

Thyroid

Heart

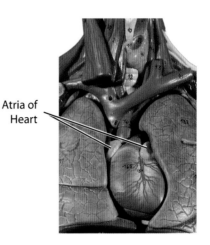

Atria of Heart

Pancreas and Intestines

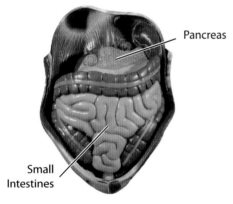

Pancreas

Small Intestines

Kidneys and Adrenal Glands

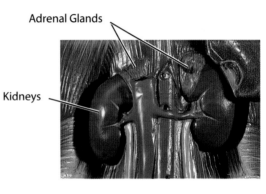

Adrenal Glands

Kidneys

Adrenal Glands, Kidneys, Pancreas, Small Intestines

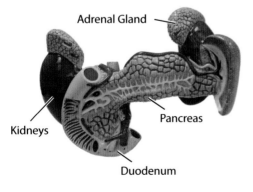

Adrenal Gland

Kidneys

Pancreas

Duodenum

Ovaries and Testes

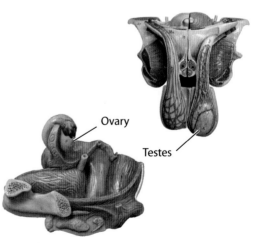

Ovary

Testes

Pancreas, Parathyroid, and Thyroid - Histology

Pancreas

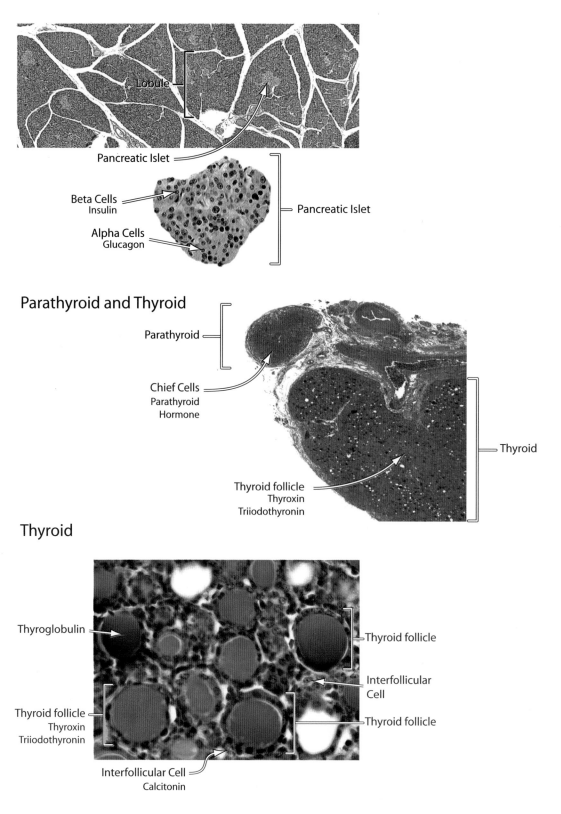

Lobule

Pancreatic Islet

Beta Cells
Insulin

Alpha Cells
Glucagon

Pancreatic Islet

Parathyroid and Thyroid

Parathyroid

Chief Cells
Parathyroid
Hormone

Thyroid

Thyroid follicle
Thyroxin
Triiodothyronin

Thyroid

Thyroglobulin

Thyroid follicle

Interfollicular
Cell

Thyroid follicle
Thyroxin
Triiodothyronin

Thyroid follicle

Interfollicular Cell
Calcitonin

Adrenal and Pituitary Gland - Histology

Adrenal Gland

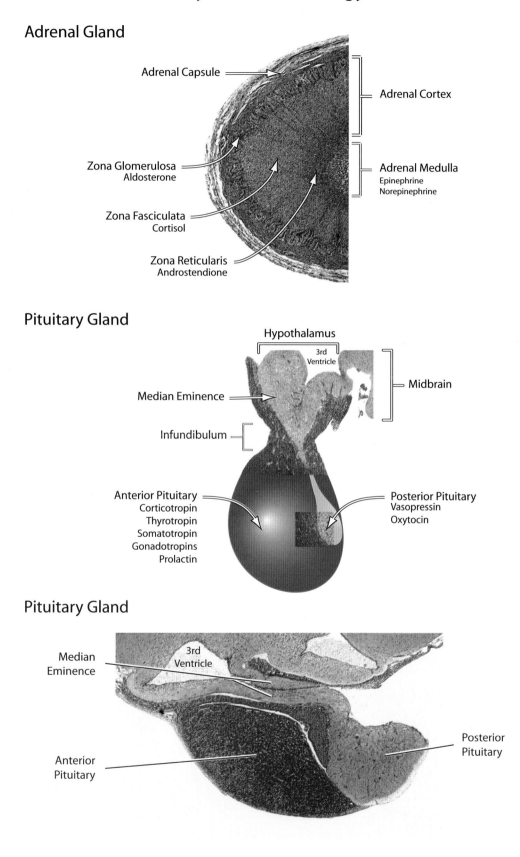

Adrenal Capsule

Adrenal Cortex

Zona Glomerulosa
Aldosterone

Adrenal Medulla
Epinephrine
Norepinephrine

Zona Fasciculata
Cortisol

Zona Reticularis
Androstendione

Pituitary Gland

Hypothalamus

3rd
Ventricle

Midbrain

Median Eminence

Infundibulum

Anterior Pituitary
Corticotropin
Thyrotropin
Somatotropin
Gonadotropins
Prolactin

Posterior Pituitary
Vasopressin
Oxytocin

Pituitary Gland

Median
Eminence

3rd
Ventricle

Posterior
Pituitary

Anterior
Pituitary

Hypothalamus and Pituitary

Posterior Pituitary

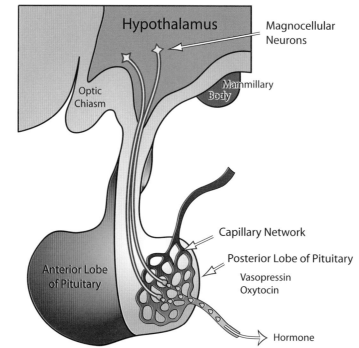

Magnocelular neurons secrete vasopressin or oxytocin directly into capillaries in the posterior lobe of the pituitary

Hypothalamus

Magnocellular Neurons

Optic Chiasm

Mammillary Body

Capillary Network

Posterior Lobe of Pituitary

Vasopressin
Oxytocin

Anterior Lobe of Pituitary

Hormone

Anterior Pituitary

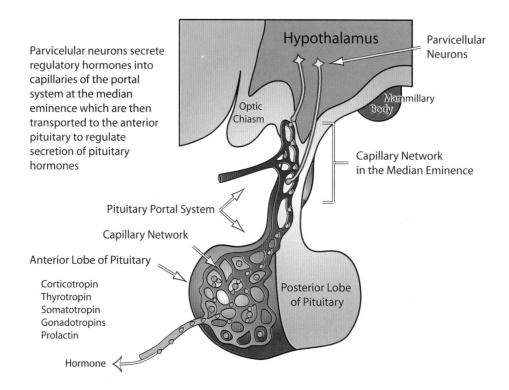

Parvicelular neurons secrete regulatory hormones into capillaries of the portal system at the median eminence which are then transported to the anterior pituitary to regulate secretion of pituitary hormones

Hypothalamus

Parvicellular Neurons

Optic Chiasm

Mammillary Body

Capillary Network in the Median Eminence

Pituitary Portal System

Capillary Network

Anterior Lobe of Pituitary

Corticotropin
Thyrotropin
Somatotropin
Gonadotropins
Prolactin

Posterior Lobe of Pituitary

Hormone

Male Reproductive Organs

Anterior

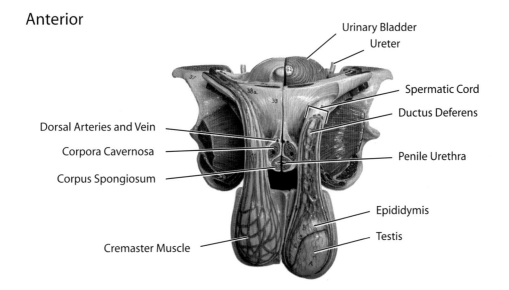

Urinary Bladder
Ureter
Spermatic Cord
Ductus Deferens
Dorsal Arteries and Vein
Corpora Cavernosa
Corpus Spongiosum
Penile Urethra
Epididymis
Cremaster Muscle
Testis

Superior

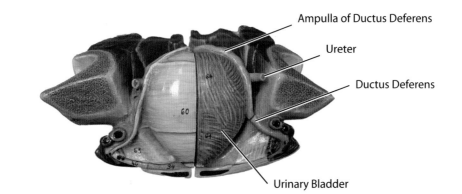

Ampulla of Ductus Deferens
Ureter
Ductus Deferens
Urinary Bladder

Posterior

Urinary Bladder
Ureter
Ampulla of Ductus Deferens
Prostate Gland
Seminal Vesicle
Scrotum
Anal Canal

Male Reproductive Organs

Midsagittal

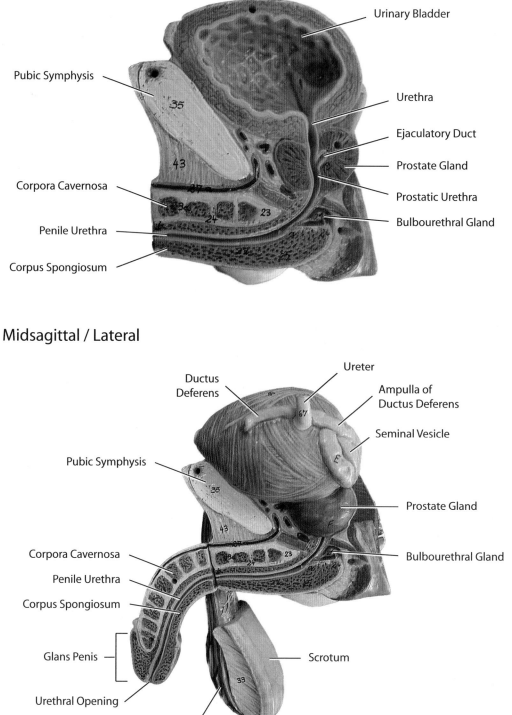

Urinary Bladder

Pubic Symphysis

Urethra

Ejaculatory Duct

Prostate Gland

Prostatic Urethra

Corpora Cavernosa

Penile Urethra

Bulbourethral Gland

Corpus Spongiosum

Midsagittal / Lateral

Ductus Deferens

Ureter

Ampulla of Ductus Deferens

Seminal Vesicle

Pubic Symphysis

Prostate Gland

Corpora Cavernosa

Penile Urethra

Bulbourethral Gland

Corpus Spongiosum

Glans Penis

Scrotum

Urethral Opening

Cremaster Muscle

Testes and Penis - Histology

Seminiferous Tubules

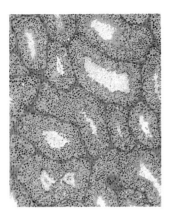

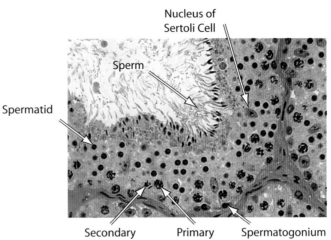

Nucleus of
Sertoli Cell

Sperm

Spermatid

Secondary
Spermatocyte

Primary
Spermatocyte

Spermatogonium

Seminiferous Tubules

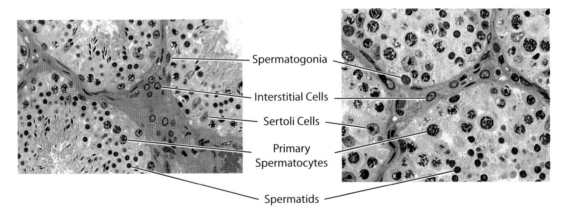

Spermatogonia

Interstitial Cells

Sertoli Cells

Primary
Spermatocytes

Spermatids

Sperm

Penis

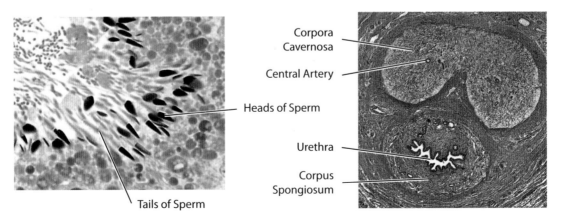

Heads of Sperm

Tails of Sperm

Corpora
Cavernosa

Central Artery

Urethra

Corpus
Spongiosum

Female Reproductive Organs

Ovary - sectioned

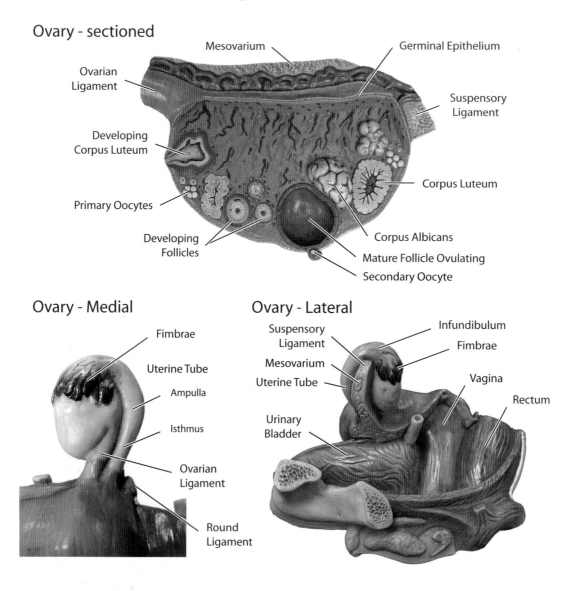

Mesovarium

Germinal Epithelium

Ovarian Ligament

Suspensory Ligament

Developing Corpus Luteum

Corpus Luteum

Primary Oocytes

Corpus Albicans

Developing Follicles

Mature Follicle Ovulating

Secondary Oocyte

Ovary - Medial

Fimbrae

Uterine Tube

Ampulla

Isthmus

Ovarian Ligament

Round Ligament

Ovary - Lateral

Suspensory Ligament

Infundibulum

Mesovarium

Fimbrae

Uterine Tube

Vagina

Urinary Bladder

Rectum

Ovaries and Uterus

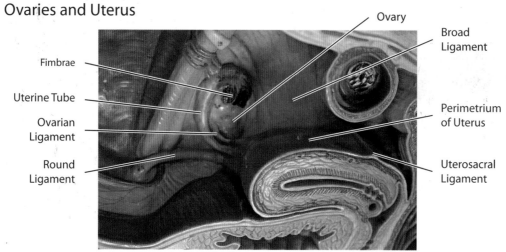

Ovary

Broad Ligament

Fimbrae

Uterine Tube

Ovarian Ligament

Perimetrium of Uterus

Round Ligament

Uterosacral Ligament

Female Reproductive Organs - with Histology

Midsagittal

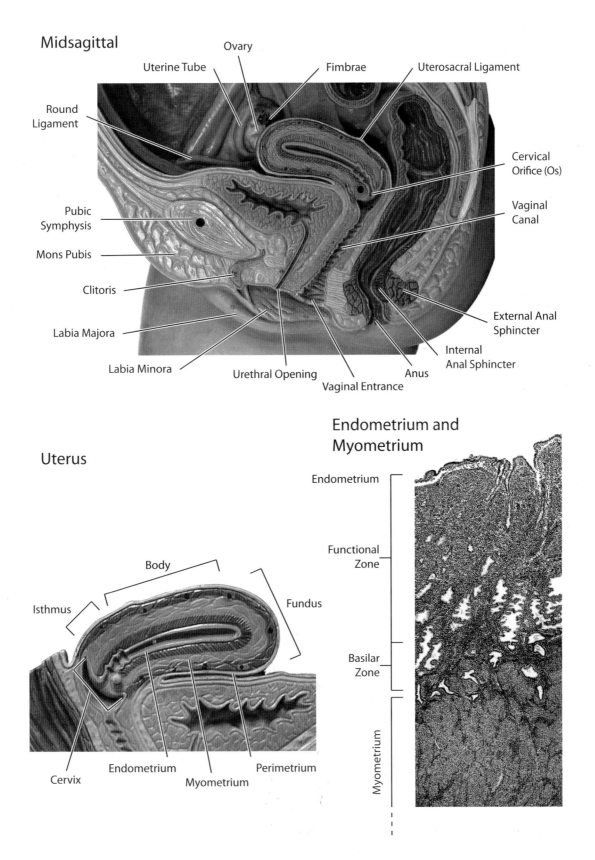

Ovary

Uterine Tube

Fimbrae

Uterosacral Ligament

Round Ligament

Cervical Orifice (Os)

Pubic Symphysis

Vaginal Canal

Mons Pubis

Clitoris

Labia Majora

External Anal Sphincter

Internal Anal Sphincter

Labia Minora

Urethral Opening

Anus

Vaginal Entrance

Uterus

Endometrium and Myometrium

Endometrium

Functional Zone

Basilar Zone

Body

Fundus

Isthmus

Myometrium

Cervix

Endometrium

Myometrium

Perimetrium

Oocytes, Ovarian Follicles, and Corpus Luteum - Histology

Primary Oocytes

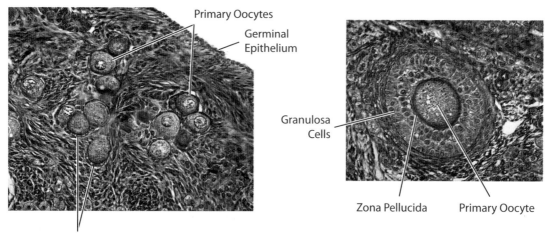

Primary Oocytes

Germinal Epithelium

Squamous Epithelial Cells around Oocytes

Developing Follicle

Granulosa Cells

Zona Pellucida

Primary Oocyte

Mature Follicle

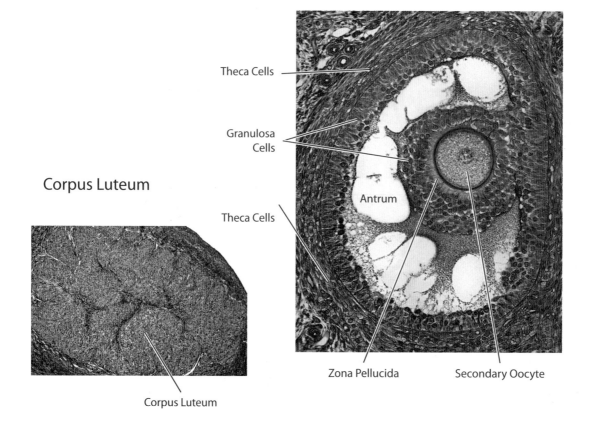

Theca Cells

Granulosa Cells

Theca Cells

Antrum

Zona Pellucida

Secondary Oocyte

Corpus Luteum

Corpus Luteum

Index

Cuspid, 6-9
Cystic Duct, 6-13
Cytosol, 1-2

D

Dead Cells, 1-5
Deep Femoral Artery, 5-14
Deltoid, 3-8, 3-9, 3-11, 3-12
Deltoid Tuberosity, 2-14
Dendrite, 1-7, 4-1, 4-2, 4-3
Dendrite / Receptor, 4-2
Dendritic Spines, 4-1
Dense (Compact) Bone, 1-6, 2-1, 2-3
Dense Irregular Fibrous, 1-6
Dense Regular Fibrous, 1-6
Denticulate Ligament, 4-9
Dentin, 6-8
Depressor Anguli, 3-5
Depressor Labii, 3-5
Dermal, 1-8, 1-9, 1-11
Dermal Papilla, 1-8, 1-9, 1-11
Dermatomes, 4-11
Dermatomes and Stretch Reflex, 4-11
Dermis, 1-1, 1-6, 1-8, 1-9, 1-10, 1-11
Dermis of skin, 1-6
Descending Aorta, 5-13
Descending Artery and Vein, 5-14
Descending Colon, 6-11
Descending Nephron Loop:, 6-21
Developing Bone, 2-3
Developing Corpus Luteum, 7-16
Developing Follicle, 7-16, 7-18
Diaphragm, 5-3, 5-4, 6-4
Diaphragm Muscle, 3-10
Diaphysis, 2-2
Digastricus - Anterior Belly, 3-6
Digastricus - Posterior Belly, 3-6
Digital Arteries, 5-12
Digits, 4-13
Disaccharidase, 6-11
Distal Convoluted Tubule:, 6-21
Distal Phalanges (1-5), 2-16, 2-20
Distal Tubule, 6-20, 6-22
Distal tubule of kidney, 1-4
Dopamine, 7-8
Dorsal Artery and Vein, 7-13
Dorsalis Pedis Artery, 5-14
Duct, 6-13
Ductus Deferens, 7-13, 7-14
Duodenal Ampulla, 6-13
Duodenal Gland, 6-16, 6-17
Duodenal Glands, 6-17
Duodenum, 6-11, 6-13, 6-17, 7-2, 7-4, 7-8, 7-9
Dura Mater, 4-8, 4-9, 4-10, 4-12, 4-18
Dural Sinuses, 4-12

E

Ear, 4-21
Efferent arteriole, 6-20
Ejaculatory Duct, 7-14
Elastic Connective Tissue, 6-5
Elastic Lamina, 5-16
Elastin, 1-6
Enamel, 6-8
Encapsulated Ending, 4-20
Encapsulated Receptors, 4-20
Endocardium of heart, 1-4, 5-10
Endocrine Glands, 7-5, 7-9
Endolymph, 4-23
Endometrium, 7-17
Endomysium, 3-2, 3-3, 3-4, 5-10, 5-16
Endoneurium, 4-4, 4-5
Endosteum, 2-2, 2-3
Endothelial Cells, 5-17
Endothelium, 5-15, 5-16
Enteric Neurons, 6-15, 6-17
Enterocrinin, 7-8
Eosinophil, 5-18, 5-19
Epicardium, 5-10
Epidermis, 1-5, 1-8, 1-9, 1-10, 1-11
Epididymis, 7-13
Epimysium, 3-2
Epinephrine, 7-8, 7-11
Epineurium, 4-5
Epiphyseal Line, 2-2
Epiphyseal Plate, 2-4
Epiphyseal Spongy Bone, 2-4, 2-5
Epiphysis, 2-2
Epithelial Tissues, 1-4, 1-5
Epithelium - Fluorescence, 6-14
Erythrocyte, 5-1, 5-17, 5-18, 5-19
Erythropoietin, 7-8
Esophagus, 6-8, 6-10, 6-14
Esophagus - Fluorescence, 6-14
Estrogen, 7-8
Ethmoid Bone, 2-6, 2-8, 2-9, 6-2
Extensor Carpi Radialis Brevis, 3-12, 3-13
Extensor Carpi Radialis Longus, 3-12, 3-13
Extensor Carpi Ulnaris, 3-12, 3-13
Extensor Digitorum, 3-12, 3-13, 3-14, 3-15, 3-16
Extensor Digitorum Longus, 3-14, 3-15, 3-16
Extensor Digitorum Minimi, 3-12, 3-13
Extensor Hallucis Longus, 3-15
Extensor Pollicis Brevis, 3-12, 3-13
Extensor Pollicis Longus, 3-12, 3-13
External Acoustic Canal, 2-7, 2-10
External Anal Sphincter, 7-17, 6-12
External Auditory Canal, 4-21
External Carotid Artery, 5-11
External Elastic Lamina, 5-16
External Iliac Artery and Vein, 5-13, 5-14
External Intercostal, 3-8, 3-10

External Nares, 6-2
External Oblique, 3-9, 3-10
Extracellular Fluid, 1-2
Extrinsic Eye Muscles, 3-7
Eye, 4-13, 4-24, 4-25, 7-2, 7-4
Eye sockets, 2-6

F

Face, 4-13
Facet for Clavicle, 2-12
Facet for Rib, 2-12
Facial and Vestibulocochlear Nerve, 4-18
Facial Nerve, 4-14, 4-17
False Ribs (#8-10), 2-12
Falx Cerebri, 4-12, 4-18
Fascicle, 3-2, 3-4, 4-5
Fatty acids, 5-18
Female, 7-2, 7-4, 7-16, 7-17
Female Reproductive Organs, 7-16, 7-17
Femoral Artery, 5-14
Femoral Artery and Vein, 5-14
Femoral Nerve, 4-7
Femur, 2-18, 2-21
Fibrinogen, 5-18
Fibroblast, 1-6
Fibrous Connective Tissue, 1-1
Fibula, 2-20, 2-21
Fibular Articular Surface, 2-19
Fibular Ligament, 2-21
Fibularis Brevis, 3-14, 3-15, 3-16, 3-17
Fibularis Longus, 3-14, 3-15, 3-16, 3-17
Filtration, 6-21
Filum Terminale, 4-8
Fimbrae, 4-14, 4-19, 7-16, 7-17
Flexor Carpi Radialis, 3-12, 3-13
Flexor Carpi Ulnaris, 3-12, 3-13
Flexor Digitorum Brevis, 3-17
Flexor Digitorum Longus, 3-15, 3-16, 3-17
Flexor Digitorum Profundus, 3-13
Flexor Digitorum Superficialis, 3-12, 3-13
Flexor Hallucis Longus, 3-17
Flexor Pollicis Longus, 3-12, 3-13
Floating Ribs (#11, 12), 2-12
Foot, 2-20, 4-13
Foramen Lacerum, 2-8, 2-9, 2-10
Foramen Magnum, 2-7, 2-8, 2-10
Foramen Ovale, 2-8, 2-9
Foramen Rotundum, 2-8, 2-9
Foramen Spinosum, 2-8, 2-9
Forearm, 4-13
Fornix, 4-14, 4-15, 4-19
Fossa Ovale, 5-8
Fovea, 4-24, 4-25
Free Nerve Ending, 4-20
Free ribosomes, 1-2
Frequency Response, 4-21

Frontal belly of Occipitofrontalis, 3-5
Frontal Bone, 2-6, 2-7, 2-8, 2-9, 6-2
Frontal Lobe, 4-12, 4-18
Frontal Sinus, 2-8, 6-2
Frontalis, 3-5
Functional Zone, 7-17
Fundus, 6-10
Fundus of Uterus, 7-17
Fused Vesicle Channels, 5-17

G

Gallbladder, 6-13
Ganglion, 4-10
Gastric Artery, 5-13
Gastric Glands, 6-15
Gastric pepsin, 6-10
Gastric Pits, 6-15
Gastric Vein, 5-13
Gastrin, 7-8
Gastrocnemius Lateral Head, 3-14, 3-15, 3-16, 3-17
Gastrocnemius Medial Head, 3-14, 3-15, 3-16, 3-17
Gemellus Inferioris, 3-17
Gemellus Internus, 3-17
Gemellus Superioris, 3-17
Genioglossus, 3-6
Geniohyoid, 3-6
Germinal Epithelium, 7-16, 7-18
Ghrelin, 7-8
Glandular Epithelium, 1-2, 1-5, 1-10
Glans Penis, 7-14
Glenoid Fossa, 2-13
Glial Cells, 1-7, 4-4
Globulins, 5-18
Globus Pallidus, 4-16, 4-19
Glomerular Capillaries, 6-20, 6-22
Glomerulus, 6-22
Glossopharyngeal Nerve, 4-14, 4-17, 4-18
Glottis, 6-3
Glucagon, 7-8, 7-10
Glucose, 5-18
Glucose Dependent Insulinotropic Hormone, 7-8
Gluteal Tuberosity, 2-18
Gluteus Maximus, 3-14, 3-15, 3-16
Gluteus Medius, 3-14, 3-15, 3-16, 3-17
Goblet Cells, 1-5, 6-1, 6-16
Golgi Complex, 1-2
Gonadal Artery, 5-13, 5-14
Gonadotropin Releasing Hormone, 7-8
Gonadotropins, 7-8, 7-11, 7-12
Gracilis, 3-14, 3-15, 3-16, 3-17
Granular Leukocytes, 5-18
Granulosa Cells, 7-18
Gray Ramus, 7-6
Great Cardiac Vein, 5-7, 5-9
Great Saphenous Vein, 5-14
Greater Curvature, 6-10

Tympanic Membrane, 4-21
Type 2 Alveolar Cells, 6-5

U

Ulna, 2-15
Ulnar Artery and Vein, 5-12
Unipolar (Sensory) Neuron, 4-2
Upper Body, 5-2
Upper Esophageal Sphincter, 6-8
Upper Jaw, 6-9
Ureter, 6-19, 6-22, 7-2, 7-4, 7-13, 7-14
Urethra, 7-14, 7-15
Urethral Opening, 7-14, 7-17
Urinary Bladder, 6-19, 7-2, 7-4, 7-13, 7-14, 7-16
Urinary Tract, 6-19
Uterine Tube, 7-16, 7-17
Uterosacral Ligament, 7-16, 7-17
Uterus, 7-16, 7-17
Utricle and Saccule, 4-23
Uvula, 6-2, 6-8

V

Vagina, 7-16
Vaginal Canal, 7-17
Vaginal Entrance, 7-17
Vagus Nerve, 4-14, 4-17, 4-18
Vas Deferens, 7-13
Vasoactive Intestinal Peptide, 7-8
Vasopressin, 7-8, 7-11, 7-12
Vastus Lateralis, 3-14, 3-15, 3-16, 3-17
Vastus Medialis, 3-14, 3-15, 3-16, 3-17
Vein, 5-15, 5-16
Ventricles of Heart, 5-4, 5-5, 5-6, 5-7, 5-8
Ventricles of Brain, 4-16
Venule, 5-15, 5-17
Vermis, 4-14, 4-15
Vertebrae, 2-11
Vertebral Artery, 5-11
Vertebral Foramen, 2-11
Vesicles, 1-2
Vestibular Apparatus, 4-23
Vestibular Duct, 4-21
Vestibular Fold, 6-3
Vestibular Ganglion, 4-23
Vestibular Membrane, 4-21, 4-22, 4-23
Vestibular Nerve, 4-23
Vestibulocochlear Nerve, 4-14, 4-17, 4-21
VII cranial nerve, 7-2
Villus, 6-16
Visceral Epithelium, 6-20
Visceral Pleura, 6-4, 6-5
Visual Cortex, 4-13
Vitreous Humor, 4-24, 4-25
Vocal Fold, 6-3
Vomer Bone, 2-6, 2-7, 2-10, 6-2

W

Wall of Stomach, 6-15
Wall of Duodenum, 6-17
Water, 5-18
Water channels, 6-21
White Blood Cells, 5-18
White Ramus, 7-6

X

X cranial nerve, 7-2
Xiphoid Process, 2-12

Z

Z-line, 3-3, 3-4
Z-line to Z-line, 3-4
Zona Fasciculata, 7-11
Zona Glomerulosa, 7-11
Zona Pellucida, 7-18
Zona Reticularis, 7-11
Zone of overlap, 3-3
Zygomatic Bone, 2-6, 2-7, 2-9
Zygomatic Process of Temporal Bone, 2-7, 2-10
Zygomaticus Major, 3-5